DATE DUE

ABRAHAM'S CHILDREN

Israel's Young Generation

Also by Peter Sichrovsky:

Strangers in Their Own Land

Born Guilty

Peter Sichrovsky

ABRAHAM'S CHILDREN

Israel's Young Generation

Translated from the German by
Jean Steinberg

Pantheon Books

New York

Library of Congress Cataloging-in-Publication Data
Sichrovsky, Peter, 1947–
[Die Kinder Abrahams. English]
Abraham's children : Israel's young generation / Peter Sichrovsky.
p. cm.
Translation of: Die Kinder Abrahams.
1. National characteristics, Israeli. 2. Israelis—Interviews.
3. Israel—Politics and government—Public opinion. 4. Jewish-Arab
relations—1973– —Public opinion. 5. Public opinion—Israel.
I. Title.
DS102.95.S5713 1991
956.94—dc20   91-12110
ISBN 0-679-40419-8

Book Design by Fritz Metsch

Manufactured in the United States of America

First American Edition

CONTENTS

PREFACE

Because I had grown up in postwar Vienna as the son of
Jewish emigrants who had survived the Nazis in a foreign
country, my relationship to Israel was as problematic to
me as it was to those among whom I lived, though for
different reasons. My family had returned to Vienna from
London as early as 1945, and many people could not understand how Jews could voluntarily go back to the cradle
of the recent insanity. My father had served in the British
army, and my mother had worked as a nurse in London
during the war, so why hadn't they stayed on in England,
or gone to Israel? Why to Vienna, of all places?

There are no easy answers. My father's family had lived
in Austria for generations, and my mother's had moved
back and forth between Vienna and Prague. My parents,
filled with the optimistic hope that the new Austria would
be different from the one they had fled, longed for the
cultural setting that had nurtured them. Back then, at the
end of the war, Israel, that faraway home of the Jews,
seemed as alien to them as to non-Jewish Austrians.

· · ·

After repeated visits to Israel I decided to write a book about that country's young generation similar to my books of interviews with the children of Jewish survivors and of Nazis.

Having spent my formative years among German-speaking Jews who were not all that different from their non-Jewish neighbors, I was not prepared for the population mix in Israel, all those diverse national backgrounds and cultures, that colorful mosaic that makes up the total picture. These men and women all have Israeli passports, and if they've lived there long enough, they generally though not invariably speak the same language. Yet they bring with them a cultural heritage as diverse as the tales of the Arabian Nights, the stories of the Brothers Grimm, the novels of Dostoevski. They are German philosophers, Siberian bear hunters, Arabian tellers of tales, African medicine men, American pop singers, and all too often all these rolled into one; yet the dominant force and influence is American.

In choosing the subjects of my interviews I sought to capture this variety. The mixture in this volume covers a wide area, from newcomers to third-generation residents, but regardless of their background, Israelis are always ready to talk, to tell the story of their families and their lives. And all of them are preoccupied with the political situation, with internal economic problems and external threats. These young Israelis are not like the old fighters of the founding generation. They travel abroad, they come into contact with people who live in peace and prosperity, and they envy what they see. They too want a minimum of well-being and security, jobs that allow them to support a family—and most of all, an end to war.

These interviews and the ideas expressed in them are not necessarily representative of the whole of Israeli society, but they do offer a cross-section of opinions and family histories.

Many immigrants live in national enclaves, in cultural and linguistic ghettos, and their national backgrounds tend to buttress long-standing prejudices and racist practices. The Ashkenazim and Sephardim, that is, the Europeans and the Orientals, are still the two main groups, and even though both are Jews they have major problems with each other. By and large Israelis look upon marriages between "Orientals" and "Europeans" as mixed marriages.

I met most of the young women and men I interviewed by chance, some in the homes of friends, others through friends of friends, and still others because they got in touch with me. And almost all were eager to talk. One of the bonds that unites modern Israelis is a deep-rooted cultural tradition of remembering and re-creating the past.

Were it not for war and the external dangers Israel faces, the country could be a veritable paradise, a place where millions of Jews (and Arabs as well) of different cultures, traditions, and languages could live, not as in a melting pot reduced to gray uniformity, but like the tiles in a mosaic, retaining their individuality yet forming a single entity.

When I was conducting the interviews that make up this book rockets from Iraq were not yet falling on Israel, threatening lives and wiping out entire sections of Tel Aviv. The exploding rockets maimed people and destroyed property, yet there was no panic. Only when Saddam Hussein proclaimed that he would not hesitate to use chemical weapons did panic become widespread. The possibility of death by gas evoked horrifying memories. No previous attack by any of Israel's Arab neighbors equaled the impact of this brutal threat. I happened to be in Israel during this period, and night after night I sat in a sealed-off room, a gas mask over my face, along with everyone else—old and young, Arabs and Jews.

These relatively harmless rockets from Iraq emphasized the deep divisions within Israel, a split that symbolizes the country's transition from its pioneer past to the present day. To stay or to leave was not an idle topic of discussion; it was a reality every family had to face up to sooner or later. Patriotic pride ran up against the fear that you yourself, and even more unthinkable, your children, might be killed by poison gas, and conflicting emotions rent many a family. Some left, but most stayed despite the threat and the danger. These differing reactions did not in fact surprise me. They echoed in many ways the full range of strongly held, controversial opinions about the life and future of Israel in the interviews that follow.

ABRAHAM'S CHILDREN

Israel's Young Generation

YAKOV

My parents had come to Israel from Libya in 1952. More than thirty thousand Jews left Libya during those years, part of the half million Jews that left the Arab countries, all of them Sephardim.

In Israel they call us blacks, in contrast to the Ashkenazim, the whites. All of us who came from the Arab countries at that time are looked on as dark-skinned, rather primitive and uncivilized savages, not like those civilized Europeans. It doesn't matter if a particular Algerian is a university professor and a Pole a beggar. It's assumed that the one is cultured and the other isn't. Mixed marriages? Do you have any idea what it means here to have a mixed marriage? I'm not talking about a marriage between a Jew and a Gentile. No, I mean a marriage of Jews, one black and the other white. That's a mixed marriage.

My father learned shoemaking in Libya. He came of a middle-class family. His parents owned a small distillery that made arrack and other spirits of that region. I know practically nothing about my mother's background. My parents came here soon after they married. At that time all immigrants were sent to big collection centers. They couldn't choose where they wanted to settle. The Jewish Agency, the authority overseeing immigration, told them where to go. My parents were sent to Pardes Hana, a small town in the middle of the country, nothing but a few huts with tin roofs in an orange grove, a so-called moshav. Unlike the collective kibbutzim, the moshavim were labor settlements, typical for the Oriental immigrants—working communes without any definite ideological orientation. The left-wing kibbutzim didn't want any blacks. They were elitists and not eager to take any of us in. Those leftists liked to talk of a new society, but reality was something else.

In the moshav my parents' life was uneventful. Father worked in construction and Mother initially stayed home. Later she took a nursing course and went to work in an old-age home.

We are four brothers and one sister. I'm the oldest. Ours was always a traditional home, even if not particularly pious. We took religious traditions seriously but we didn't keep all the laws, although over the years this has changed. Lately Mother has become more and more religious; Father still hasn't quite made up his mind. He observes the Sabbath, but when the weather is good and the sea is calm he forgets about observance and goes fishing. We children are not religious. The family was always tolerant about differences in our practices. We didn't criticize each other; we observed our religion whichever way we chose. Basically, religion never became an issue, in contrast to other families, where differences and problems are common. As a matter of fact, in many families I know the problem is the reverse of ours: parents who are gradually loosening their ties to religion, drawing away from the rigid piety of their parents, while the children become more pious, more critical of their parents, insisting on rigid observance of religious decrees. The family of one of my friends is representative of all trends: a grandfather who was a rabbi, a left-wing father in a kibbutz who believes in the world revolution, and a daughter who became religious and married an Orthodox Jew. I once visited them when all three generations were present. The fight that broke out was Israel's history during the last forty years in a nutshell.

My parents moved to Netanya, a small town north of Tel Aviv, before I was born. We lived in a very modest working-class section, on one of its better streets. It was a block of small houses with front yards, rather unusual for this section, amid big apartment blocks.

The population there was almost exclusively Sephardic working-class. Those were the real slums, a ghetto of blacks. Only Orientals lived there. The schools weren't as good as elsewhere, nor the housing. Their life, I guess, was something like the way blacks live in America. And like them they also had an organization calling itself Black Panthers, a group of Sephardic revolutionaries—or maybe they were only protesters. Still, they were successful in publicizing the situation of the Sephardim. Gradually their housing as well as their schools improved. At some point the whites learned to accept the blacks as fellow human beings, and above all as Jews. I went to elementary school in that section. Mother wanted us to learn a trade just as soon as we got out of school, but Father did his best to persuade us to get an education, so we would have a chance to better ourselves.

During my vacation I often went with Father to his construction site to help out and earn a little money. That experience was enough to convince me that I didn't want to follow in his footsteps. I was going to learn something. I didn't want to be just a laborer.

My brother and I were the only ones to finish college.

The others graduated from high school and took up a trade. When I was fourteen I had the choice of going to a regular high school or to a military boarding school. If you enroll in such a boarding school you have to commit yourself to serving a minimum of five years in the army. This was three years after the Six-Day War, and everybody was proud of the army. I was no exception. I too wanted to be a hero in uniform.

Fortunately—now I can say fortunately—I didn't pass the entrance exam. Instead, I enrolled in a high school in Netanya. At the time it seemed almost like a disgrace. An army career was the dream not only of all boys but of many parents as well. Service in the military meant good pay, a respected position, and, in case of early retirement —at about age forty-five—a sizable separation payment. Today I see these things differently, as do many of my friends and contemporaries. The army no longer is what it used to be. A fighting force that had been the guarantor of our survival now often behaves like an aggressive, brutal gang. All you have to do is look around and you'll see what I mean.

I used to be fascinated by technology and the natural sciences, and at high school I concentrated on biology. I thought I'd study either chemistry or biology or medicine. I remember that shortly before graduation I wrote down that I wanted to become a pilot or a painter or a doctor or a chemist. Those were the idealized professions. Every boy put down "pilot." To fly a plane in the Israeli army was the absolute dream of all of them.

High school brought a great change into my life. I now met children from different social backgrounds, not only the working-class children from our district. Even so, the kids I became friends with came from simple homes, boys who wanted to get an education and make something of themselves. I had little contact with the richer kids.

Israel has always had two problems: social class and ethnic background. Frequently the two were linked. The Ashkenazim, the whites, not only were reputed to be more cultured, but, even more important, they had more money. We, the blacks, were the poor, the simple folk, the Arabs without culture and without money. In school I sat next to a boy whose parents had come from Germany. I think their name was something like Goldenberg. I once was invited to his house. I couldn't believe my eyes: huge rooms lined with bookcases, and his father wore a suit and a straw hat, even indoors. We all wore school uniforms, but somehow the children of the rich still managed to look different.

A year after the Yom Kippur War, having finished school, I was called into the army. At the time I still had the urge, perhaps not quite as strongly as at age fourteen, to be a combat soldier. At any rate, I wanted to become an officer, and even considered signing up for an extra year of duty after finishing my three-year stint. The desire to become part of the glorious history of the country also played a part. Europeans may be proud of their Beethoven and their Shakespeare, but here soldiers are the folk heroes, and their heroism is connected with how many enemies they have killed.

It didn't take long before I realized that this system wasn't for me. Once you're on the inside everything looks different. There was nothing glorious about this army. That rigid system didn't appeal to me one bit. I had trouble taking orders, and so I tried for the impossible—to become a training instructor. Basic training, that's how soldiers spend the first four weeks of their life in the military. I tried to make myself as small, as unobtrusive as possible; my only aspiration was to get done with these three years as quickly and with as few problems as I could.

In retrospect, I must say that these were perhaps the three most pointless years of my life. Going home for week-ends from camp, I had to pass through Jerusalem to catch the military bus. To this day I can't stand Jerusalem. The place where we got the bus that brought us back to camp for another week is still hateful to me. Whenever I pass it I relive the depression of those days, and I connect this feeling of depression with Jerusalem, not with the euphoria of the Six-Day War when we retook Jerusalem. The Yom Kippur War changed a lot of things. When I entered the army, being a "little head"—that's what people like me were called—was becoming a popular ploy. What it meant was "Don't call attention to yourself, don't do more than you're ordered to, don't volunteer."

When I got out of the army I took two months off to work in a filling station to make money for my education. That's when I began to get interested in computers and decided to study communications. I took all sorts of jobs to make a little money: tutoring, airport security guard, any old thing. Father offered to help me out financially, but I didn't want to take anything from him. I knew how hard my parents had worked, and also, back then it wasn't all that difficult to pick up some extra money while going to school. I preferred to make it on my own rather than let my parents help me. They still had four younger children at home to take care of.

At school I lived in a dorm, where I shared a room with an Israeli Druse. The guys in the room next to us were also Druse. Up to then I'd hardly had any contacts with Druse, and in the beginning it was all very fascinating.

We got along well, ate together, and had lively political discussions.

The two Druse next door were violently pro-Arab, and we were forever arguing about who had done what to whom, the Israelis to the Palestinians or vice versa. Our discussions were rhetorical battles. We didn't try to persuade each other; we just wanted to come up with the best arguments. But our friendly relations broke off abruptly one day when they told me that they belonged to a group affiliated with the PLO. Back then it was unthinkable for me to be in contact with, or even speak to, someone connected with the PLO. It was not simply a matter of right or left. I was a right-winger, an uncritical supporter of the Israeli position. Speaking to Arabs was out of the question, and as far as I was concerned, the PLO was a band of criminals. It's hard to believe how much I have changed.

Ethnic background or social class never was a consideration when I thought of whom I might one day marry. I never inquire into the ethnic background of other people. I don't care whether someone is black or white. That's got nothing to do with either a person's character or intelligence. And my parents didn't attach any importance to it either. They were prepared to accept my choice of a wife. The old family traditions also weren't important to me. When I was ready to start my own family what was going to matter to me was the individual, the woman, regardless of where she was from.

Of course there are ties to the past. I might perhaps even be interested in seeing the city my parents came from in Libya, the place where they used to live. But that doesn't mean that I would carry on the traditions of my parents.

When I first met my wife her parents disapproved of me. They were typical whites, Ashkenazim, even though they came from Hungary. But they were proud of their culture. They thought of themselves as somewhat German, European. I knew that these were nothing but prejudices and that I would be able to win them over. We now have a very good relationship. But my wife and I would have married anyway, whether or not our parents approved. And even though her father was opposed to our marriage, one day he dropped the hint that if his daughter and I were considering marrying he'd accept it.

But the gossip in his family didn't stop. Even at our wedding some whispers could be heard: "Couldn't she have found someone else? Did it have to be a black?" I had never before been confronted so directly with this sort of prejudice. Neither at school nor at work did I ever feel disadvantaged because of my ethnic background. Because of my social class, perhaps. The children of rich parents don't have to work to pay for their education. But that has nothing to do with ethnicity. The parents of two of my fellow students had a fruit stand across the street from the university. Their sons drove a big car and ate off fancy china. Their background was simple, but they had money.

As a security guard at the airport I often had to work all night and then in the morning go directly to the university. Naturally I envied the students who came to school after a good night's sleep and a hearty breakfast. But I never thought of it in terms of "those Ashkenazim, they have it easy." I felt that the people who had no worries and lived well had worked for it, that everybody had an even chance. That was back then. Today I know better. People who come from the right sort of family have a better chance.

My relationship to my parents hasn't changed. They're my parents, not my friends. I don't discuss my personal problems with them. There's too much distance between us.

And this land? This country? I don't know, everything's changed so much these past ten years. Before, everything was so simple. The bad Arabs on one side, the good Israelis on the other, and I was one of the good ones. But never before have I seen our society as split as now. I never used to get so upset over what our government did as I do now.

Since the war in Lebanon, in which I served, everything has changed. Before, I had never thought about whether or not a war was just. Since I disliked everything about the army anyway, I didn't think too much about the causes of war. I had a strong aversion to everything military, but my distaste wasn't based on ideological or political considerations.

Now, particularly since this conflict, and also since my own annual reserve duty, I have become more and more antimilitaristic. I hate this reserve duty. I'd do anything to get out of it. Every year I try to come up with new excuses, with reasons why I can't serve. I even prefer paying the two-hundred-shekel fine to reporting on time.

I've seen service in the occupied territories, and I hate having to go against the local population. I used to hate the Arabs, although I didn't really know them. It's just that we grow up with prejudice. The Arabs are those guys in the enemy camp, in those strange outfits, who're out to kill us. They're the ones doing the dirty work; they can't be trusted. I'd always been afraid of them, afraid of a knife in the back, of being hit by a rock or having a bomb thrown at me. Always that fear. But when I saw how poor they were, how pitiful, I changed my mind. Today I no longer feel the same way about them.

I saw many things while stationed in the occupied territories. I was there when demonstrators were beaten, I was there when a family was given ten minutes to clear out of their house because it was going to be blown up. Suddenly you don't feel any hatred anymore. All I saw was women crying, and children—a family standing in front of a house containing most of their belongings, and within seconds it would all be gone. I was filled with self-loathing.

Now my politics are very different from those of my youth. I can probably be considered far left, even to the left of the Labor Party. I am in favor of negotiations with the PLO. I think it's our only chance for survival. The occupation must come to an end. This is not merely a rational political argument; I'm convinced that there is no other alternative, no other choice. We must begin to accept the idea that one day an Arab country will exist in our midst.

Today I see myself as an Israeli, not a Zionist. I accept the historical background that gave rise to Zionism, but a Zionist was someone who packed up his belongings and came to Israel. To be a Zionist in Israel is a contradiction. A land that tolerates another one next door must finally come into being, and all parties in this endless conflict must accept this.

I am proud of being a Jew, proud of Jewry's great and tragic history. But the past is the past, and today we have a Jewish state. Today I am an Israeli. That is my identity.

I used to be proud of our fighting spirit, of our national heroes who fought for their country. Today I take greater pride in our technological achievements, in the rapid strides we have made. I want to see us develop, to become a modern nation. I am more interested in our agricultural advances than in our military victories.

I would like to spend some time in Europe or the U.S.A., to study and then return to Israel to help in our development, and also profit from it. But let's finally have peace, without the military and the daily death toll.

I never want to be anything but an Israeli, and now it's possible to be a good Israeli without having to be a Zionist. Today the Zionists are the right-wingers, and the right-wingers are against peace. They think they can bring about a solution by force. What a tragic idea in so pious a country!

DINAH

I want to tell you right off the bat, I hate the Arabs. I hate them and I'm afraid of them. It's a strange combination of two conflicting feelings. Their hands are covered with the blood of my Jewish sisters and brothers. Just take a look at everything they've been doing for years. Can you blame me for being afraid of them? Are you going to tell me that these are irrational, panicky reactions? Politically, I put my trust in those who still my fears, not those who make me even more afraid. And the old Socialists no longer fill that role.

I come of a Socialist family. I was born twenty-seven years ago in Ramat-Hasharon, a middle-class suburb of Tel Aviv, a nice section of one-family houses with private gardens and well-tended lawns, and I still live there with my parents.

Both my parents were born in Israel. My grandparents had immigrated in the early thirties from Germany. Actually, only my mother's parents came from Germany. My mother's father wasn't Jewish, but he had a premonition about what was going to happen to the Jews in Germany, and he persuaded my grandmother to emigrate to Palestine.

After the war he returned to Germany, I don't remember exactly why. According to the official family version, he went back to help rebuild Germany. But I think that wasn't the only reason. Perhaps he didn't want to convert, or perhaps, not being Jewish, he never felt quite at home here.

Not a single one of our relatives was killed in the Holocaust. Thank God, the Holocaust was never a topic of discussion in our house. Our family was always well off. My grandparents had a candy factory. They came here at a time when things were being built up, when the possibilities were still great. My parents now manage that factory.

I went to school here in this suburb, and in my free time I was active in the Socialist youth movement. My parents and grandparents all were Socialists. They saw no conflict between their political allegiance and their business ideas. Back then being a Socialist meant helping build the country.

My military service was fairly uneventful. I was secretary to a high-ranking officer in Tel Aviv. After that I studied biology, and for the past three years I've been working as a laboratory technician in our municipal hospital.

A few months ago my life took a radical turn. I enrolled in a university course in the biblical and archaeological roots of this land. Israel's historical past is a subject I've been interested in for a long time. It's an area in which I would like to work professionally.

I became involved in the political life of the university, attended discussion groups and other such political gatherings. A wide range of politicians came to our meetings: left-wingers, right-wingers, liberals, all political shades, all of them defending their positions and trying to win us over to their side. I'm not one to make up my mind in a hurry; I listened to all of them. Many of them were fascinating speakers. But now, having listened to all those speeches and the often violent discussions, I've come to the conclusion that Likud has the only logical program for the future.

I admire people like Begin, Arens, and other moderate Likud politicians. I don't much care for the more radical ones like Sharon or Levi, but I realize we need them to win the support of the so-called broad masses. They are forceful, persuasive speakers. None of your rational, boring arguments; they speak to the soul of the people, above all to their fears. Because fear is the basic emotion, for me and also for others. We're afraid of the Arabs because we don't trust them, or perhaps precisely because we do believe what they say.

I'm not the only one to have changed; so have my parents. They're no longer the Socialists of the past; they've lost faith in Peres and his comrades and their pipe dreams of reconciliation.

To tell you the truth, I'm against negotiations with the PLO. They're a band of murderers, and nobody can tell me that they've changed. And you can't negotiate with criminals and murderers, with terrorists.

Perhaps the single most crucial happening that made me change my mind was Peres's announcement that he was planning to convene an international peace conference. That set off an alarm in my mind. For the first time I realized the direction the Socialists were taking. They're ready to gamble, to risk everything, just to earn the approval of other countries. They're willing to run the risk of negotiating with criminals, to have us sit down at a table with the Russians, French, and British, all of whom in their own way are against us.

In that event, what could the Americans do? If ten people are meeting, and eight of them are against us, they'll force us to negotiate with the PLO, to accept the outcomes of negotiations that will bring us endless war rather than peace. Not so the Likud. They make foreign policy not with an eye on other countries but on behalf of their own people. Since going to the university I've become active in the Likud student organization.

If my field of study weren't so interesting I wouldn't mind going into politics. One high-ranking politician has even asked me to become his secretary. Still, I prefer my scientific work. I admit to being afraid of the Arabs. Don't you think I have reason to fear? Every one of us knows a family in which someone has been murdered or hurt in a terrorist attack, or who has lost someone in a war with the Arabs.

The only politics the Arabs understand is the politics of force. When you give them a finger they take the whole hand. That, unfortunately, is their mentality, and it will never change. All of us, including me, have had personal encounters with Arabs. In my laboratory many Arabs from the territories are working in menial jobs. The only way to deal with them is by being both objective and stern. For example, just the other day, I arrived at my office earlier than usual. An Arab was washing the floor and the tables. I went to another cubicle in the rear. I didn't want to be in the same room with him. These days one has to be very careful; before you know it you can find yourself with a knife in the back. When I got back to my room I found him sitting in my chair, his feet on my desk, a cup of coffee in front of him, listening to an Arab radio broadcast. And he was going through my papers. I remained very calm even though I was boiling mad and nervous. I said to him, "Take your feet off the table and drink your coffee somewhere else. You workers have your own room where you can prepare your coffee." At first he tried to talk his way out of the situation by grinning foolishly and making some stupid excuse. I threatened to report him to the administration. That would have meant the end of his job with us. Whereupon he made himself scarce and didn't bother me. That, unfortunately, is the tone between the Arabs and us. Perhaps we are a little too tense and react to them like enemies.

I also believe that we should stop employing Arabs from the territories in Jewish establishments. The danger is too great, for the Arabs as well. How many of them have already been killed only because they wanted to work with Israelis? Besides, we have enough unemployed Jews who can do these jobs. Of course, they'd probably want more money, but that can't be helped. It's better to pay more than to have to deal with Arabs all the time.

Perhaps this sounds racist, but my only concern is peace for our country, and we can't have peace at any price. I also don't want us to withdraw from the territories. After all, according to biblical law, they belong to us.

I am not very pious—on the contrary, I don't like those religious ones, those parasites who study Torah instead of serving in the army—but I see Israel's history from the historical perspective, which tells us that this has been our land for two thousand years. However, if we should have to evacuate some of the territories I hope the settlers will not defend themselves with arms. What kind of country would we be if the army should have to fight against its own Jewish settlers?

It makes the Arabs furious to see what these settlers have made of the land, but still, I couldn't live there. I'm used to the amenities of urban life. Ideologically I can understand the settlers, but I can't imagine what their daily life must be like.

I am a confirmed Zionist, and Israel is my home. However, being a Zionist in Israel today means remembering the old fighters and preserving the continuity of that tradition. Of course, in the past it was the Socialists, men like Ben-Gurion and Levi Eshkol, who built the country. Strong, heroic, successful men. I would like to model myself on them. They are my ideals. They would never have negotiated with any Arab. They wouldn't have given an inch. They wouldn't have misunderstood the meaning of the word "peace." They stood ready to defend and recapture every inch of Jewish land.

Their logical successor today is the Likud, not the Socialist Party. Peres is a weakling. And Rabin and Navon and all those others, they're nothing but bureaucrats. All they want to do is talk, and I'm scared of what will come out of their talking. The men of my family all served in the army—my uncles, my father, they fought for this land. Am I to betray them? Should everything have been in vain?

Here in Israel we have an annual day of commemoration of the Holocaust: Yom Hashoa. Every year they try to show the children and the young people that there had been resistance when six million of us Jews were exterminated. But in fact it's useless to show something that basically never happened. All of us today live with the trauma that back then nobody defended himself. That must never happen again. Strength is something very important today here in Israel. Every show of weakness frightens us; every display of compliance reminds us of the extermination of the six million. The only reason we are living in Israel today is that for the first time in two thousand years there again exists a Jewish army that is strong, perhaps stronger than any other. I love this country, I want to stay here, I want to live here, and I despise all who leave because they can make more money or live better somewhere else where life is more pleasant.

Six months ago I visited a foreign land for the first time in my life. I went to Egypt with some fellow students. We were interested in excavations. Except for things like that, I see no reason to go to another country. This year I will also join a group for a trip through Europe, visiting archaeological sites and museums. A study trip. I prefer spending my vacations here, in my own country, where I know my way around and speak the language.

Egypt was an absolute catastrophe. The food was even worse than here, although the Sephardic influence in our country is becoming stronger. I have nothing against the Sephardim. They're Jews just like us. But I regret that the European influence hasn't been greater. I just don't like the food, the music, and the behavior of the Sephardim. Everything is so shrill. Their music is monotonous and loud, and they are noisy and inconsiderate. What happened to the European culture of us Ashkenazim? In a few years it'll all be gone. We'll be living in an Eastern country.

I would never marry a Sephardi, even a completely Europeanized one. There's always a little remnant, and you can't get around the Arab influence on them. Sephardim treat their wives like inferiors. They expect you to wait on them, they don't want you to have any interests of your own or a profession. Thanks a lot. But the influence of the religious groups on our daily life also troubles me. If things continue this way we'll soon have a Jewish Iran. In that case even I would be willing to leave. Let's hope it won't come to that.

Let's finally put the intifada down. We mustn't even dream of talking to these terrorists. Only after it's put down can we think of peace and negotiate. How can I be expected to sit down at a table with someone who has a knife in his hand under the table and only waits for me to become careless or turn my back? And who would be the leaders of the PLO, the Arabs with whom I'd have to sit at the negotiating table? They'd be the rebels, the terrorists, the leaders of the intifada. How can you believe that someone who for years thought only of killing Jews would suddenly sit down with us to talk about peaceful coexistence?

I often have the feeling that I keep on mulling these things over in my mind to reassure myself. But at other times I feel desperate and I think that these are nothing but emotional arguments that convince no one. Fear is not a persuasive argument; strength is better. Who are the people who peddle the nonsense that we no longer need to be afraid? What a stupid piece of advice! They're probably people who've never had to live with the consequences of their misjudgments. For me a peaceful Arab is one who sits before me disarmed, not one whose siren words I believe.

Politics also dominates my personal life. Actually, I no longer really have a private life. I go to an occasional movie, and I also have a boyfriend, but he doesn't really interest me a lot. Things also aren't so simple as far as men are concerned. The only boyfriend one can have is one with whom one agrees politically. The lines have been drawn so firmly. You can't compare it to Europe, where you might possibly have friends who don't vote like you. How could I have a friend who supports the Socialists, who is in favor of negotiations with the PLO? I would be in a state of constant agitation. How could I live harmoniously with such a person? It's unthinkable. And so I keep on searching, go from one to another, looking for a comrade, a political partner rather than a boyfriend. And when I do find one I discover that even though we agree politically we don't · love each other. Politics plays such a powerful role; it dominates everything. There's no such thing as halfway beliefs. I can't split myself in half and accept a man intellectually but not emotionally, or vice versa. What I'm left with, then, are brief affairs, short stories, none of which are ideal.

There comes a time when you stop dreaming and become a realist, a terribly realistic individual. I'm still living with my parents. We talk about politics and our discussions make sense. We're in agreement.

Naturally, like any other woman, I dream of having a family one day. But I don't think I can lower my standards. As a matter of fact I tend to become more and more selective. I keep on fantasizing about finding someone with whom I'm in tune politically and emotionally, and that doesn't make things any easier.

What I enjoy most of all is my work with my friends at the university, with the other Likud students. With every passing day we become more and more involved. Tel Aviv University is the only university that is still a left-wing bastion. All the others have changed. Their students are coming over to us. They believe us. Likud is the only future of this land.

We must be strong, stronger than all the others. Then we'll survive.

ELI

My parents met in a DP camp near Nuremberg. Having survived the war, both of them must have felt indescribably lonely and lost. They married in 1946. It was my father's second marriage. His first wife and child were gassed in a concentration camp. I was born in 1947, and my sister was born the next year.

When we first came to Israel, in 1949, we were housed in a center for new immigrants; later we lived in Jerusalem for a while. After that my parents were sent to a Labor Party moshav near Rehovot.

It was sheer paradise for us. I have lovely memories of that place. We children had a grand time. To this day I feel the urge to run through the fields, eat just-picked fruit and vegetables, drink a glass of milk fresh from the cow. I think for my parents it was like going from hell to heaven.

My father loved being a farmer. His tomatoes, cucumbers, onions, and all his other produce were the best. He was the first to introduce a milking machine into his cow barn. He threw himself into his work, grateful to have the opportunity to do something useful. It was like being given a second chance at life, with a new wife and a new family.

My parents, being pious, saw to my religious education.
I attended school in our village, and twice a week I traveled
to a neighboring town for religious instruction. At age
fourteen I entered a parochial trade school, studying aero-
mechanics. There, in addition to our technical training and
the regular school subjects, we had intensive religious
instruction.

But something was wrong with my personal religion. On
the outside I pretended to be pious, but inside I was completely nonbelieving. The settlement in which we lived had
been founded by the Labor Party, which meant religion
wasn't taught there. What we had instead was the Socialist
youth movement, and all of their activities took place Friday evening and Saturday, when pious people go to synagogue. I was torn between the two. On one side were all
my friends, and on the other my family and the to me
senseless observance of Sabbath laws. I'd go to synagogue
with my father, after which I'd run off to my friends in the
youth group as fast as my feet would carry me.

It is interesting to see the different roads taken by my
village and the neighboring town. Both were settled by
immigrants, mostly from Hungary and Russia and various
other European countries, and almost all of them were
observant when they first got here. In the course of time
our village became less and less religious. Fewer and fewer
people went to synagogue. Those of my contemporaries
who still live there are completely nonobservant. By contrast, the young people in the neighboring village, a community founded not by the Labor Party but by a religious
group, the Workers of Zion, are observant. The town was
a center of the religious youth movement, and religious
instruction played an important role. As I got older I began
to look on religion as a meaningless restriction on my life.

I thought all those rules obsolete, out of step with the life of modern youth. It was like a corset I was eager to strip off so I could breathe freely.

My military career made all this possible. As soon as I entered the military I began to feel like an adult standing on my own two feet, free to discard all vestiges of my religious past. Only when I visited the family, not wanting to hurt my father, did I continue to pretend to be religious. Father sensed that I was play-acting, and naturally it pained him.

I joined the air force, a logical step considering my train-ing, and there I stayed for twenty-two years. I was mad about flying. My profession became my life, and I spent far more time in the bellies of planes than at home. I took part in everything during those years: every war, every military engagement, every campaign. Strapped into my seat, almost glued to it, enclosed, alone, it was like an addiction. All those stupid clichés about flying and air com-bat are true. It gets into your blood. Sitting in a plane, war is reduced to a lonely game, though unfortunately often a deadly one.

I met my wife during my first year in the army and we married as soon as I became a professional soldier and earned a living. My wife, who like me comes from a pious family, had also moved away from religion. We now have four children; the oldest is twenty and the youngest is still in elementary school.

When I turned forty I was discharged from the military, as is the practice here. I get a monthly pension, and in addition the severance payment I received allowed me to buy into a business. As a matter of fact I invested in a number of enterprises, but never a successful one. For brief periods I was variously the part-owner of an old-age home, a paper factory, and other small businesses. However, my partners got into trouble with the tax authorities and the businesses failed. So much for my dream of becoming an entrepreneur. When my father decided to retire we moved back to my hometown and I took over the family agriculture business. Following in my father's footsteps, I once more became a farmer. After those heady years in the military, life again became peaceful and predictable.

Shortly after moving back home—that's now six years ago—my sister talked us into attending a religious retreat. At the time we looked on it as an opportunity to relax someplace at a price we could afford. All we planned to do there was to listen politely to the welcoming speeches. But we were in for a surprise. The very first lecture was so interesting that we found ourselves going to the next one and the one after that.

What was supposed to have been a relaxing vacation turned into an intensive, demanding, and fascinating educational experience. We returned home determined to put religion back into our lives, but now with a reverse twist. Instead of pretending to piety in public, as I'd done in my youth, I pretended to be irreligious, while at home we ate only kosher and observed the Sabbath, and I wore a yarmulke.

Our oldest daughter was happy over this change in our home. She had been drawn to religion since earliest childhood. She liked spending time with her grandparents and loved the religious atmosphere there. She always wanted to live like them. The other children, however, reacted very differently. The second-oldest was not all that pleased, and even now, although he attends a religious school, he is not completely convinced. The two youngest ones were too little to have been fully conscious of the change. The younger a child, the easier the adjustment. Our oldest daughter had always wanted to go to a religious school and so she had no problem with it.

We soon found out how differently the children responded to their religious instruction. At first our oldest son was so unhappy that we let him stay at the public school in town. At home we reached a compromise: he'd have Friday night dinner with the family after attending synagogue with me, and then, after the meal, he could join his young Socialist friends or go to parties. Funny how life repeats itself. Here was my son, following in my footsteps exactly.

As soon as my wife and I were sure that our rediscovered belief was not a passing phase but a permanent commitment, a turn toward a positive outlook, we decided to leave the moshav. Our fellow members were completely nonobservant, while we wanted to live among people who shared our feelings and ideas and point of view. And so we moved into a settlement in the occupied territories, mostly because of the children. More and more, they were becoming outsiders in their old neighborhood. Were it not for the children we might possibly have stayed at the moshav; life there was certainly more comfortable, especially in the beginning. Before we bought the house we're in now, the six of us lived in a space of about 150 square feet. Everybody who wants to live in this sort of settlement is initially assigned such cramped quarters in a communal dwelling. Only after the resident settlers agree to admit the newcomers, which takes at least a year, can you buy a house if one is available; if not, you're given a piece of land to build on.

We have adjusted well to life here. This is a very pleasant, close-knit community. We know one another well and have many friends. For the little ones it is paradise. There are so many children here and they can play outdoors. Lots of open space and clean air, and above all it's quiet—no city noise, no dirt. Actually we lead a very privileged existence here.

The two older children are still in touch with their friends at the moshav, but their interests have diverged. Every time my daughter comes back from a visit with her old school friends she says that she finds them very superficial, not interested in anything but clothes and parties. They bore her.

Our son, on the other hand, has remained close to his old friends and spends many a weekend with them. I'm sure that he also goes to parties with them on Friday night. I remember doing the same thing. There's no point in forcing things; it only has the opposite effect. I don't want to throw my weight around, but I see to it that his religious education isn't neglected. Naturally I hope that ultimately he will decide on behalf of religion, but I neither can nor want to press the issue.

For me and my family the decision to return to religion was the absolutely right one. I enjoy the peace of the Sabbath, the Friday evenings with the family. No rushing about, no desperate chasing after diversion and entertainment. It is like an inward journey, a trip into an isolated, quiet world. Entirely different matters suddenly take on or recede in importance. I think that leading a religious life as a religious person in a religious environment is a good way to live.

My political ideas have changed as well, not only because of my turn to religion. Ever since I seriously began to think about politics I have stood on the right. I had been a passionate adherent of the Likud all along, but now I feel they've moved too far to the left, to the position of the old Socialist Party. All of them have moved to the left, above all the Labor Party, which now stands on the extreme left.

I have always tried to take firm political stands and refused to follow vacillating politicians.

Now I support the annexation of the occupied territories. There can be no turning back. We and thousands like us live here now, just like the thousands of Arabs who live in Israel. This is a Jewish land; it now belongs to Israel. Dividing it would be madness, and also pointless. It wouldn't help anybody, least of all the Palestinians themselves. The best solution would be for the Palestinians to become Israeli citizens, with all the rights and privileges of citizens, with the right to vote, with no job discrimination and equal rights. In that event, however, they'd also have to serve in the army and pay taxes just like us.

I dream of a country with a loyal citizenry, whether they be Jews, Arabs, or Christians—and all of them Israelis. What sense would it make to divide up this tiny land? Two halves do not become stronger just because they do not yet function as a single entity. If such a state were to become reality it would have the right to make certain demands on its citizens. Those who refuse to pledge their loyalty to it, whether Jews or Arabs, ought then to be expelled from the country.

I know, all this sounds naive, but once feelings like fealty and loyalty to the state take hold, then for all I care a Palestinian could become its prime minister and we could live in peace here with our Arab neighbors.

LISA

I was born and grew up in Philadelphia, and I have nothing but bad memories. I hated that city for a variety of reasons, mainly because of our religion. We were forever outsiders—different and isolated. All our neighbors were Catholics. Not only were we the only Jews on our block, but we children were the only ones who didn't go to parochial school. We went to public school and our neighbors called us dirty Jews.

We then moved to a Jewish neighborhood, but there we didn't fit in either. The people there were more prosperous than we. And so instead of religious discrimination we experienced social snubs. It never bothered my brothers. They didn't seem to mind, but I suffered. Philadelphia was and always will be an unhappy chapter in my life. I don't care if I never see it again.

In 1969—I was then eleven—our parents announced that we were going to Israel for a year. They made it sound like a vacation: a whole year with no school, with no pressure. I should just enjoy myself, they told me, make friends and have fun. I was thrilled by the idea of going to another country, by the prospect of a whole year of freedom, not to mention leaving Philadelphia. But it was also important for me to know that America was still my home, that we'd be coming back. Father promised that we'd never stay for good in what he called that barbaric, uncultured country.

We arrived in Israel in August 1969, and from the moment we set foot there I felt good. We found a nice apartment in Haifa, with friendly neighbors, and for the first time in my life I felt we belonged. It didn't take me long to make friends and to become integrated. Things couldn't have been any better. I liked Israel, yet when Father six months later announced that we were going to settle there I felt betrayed. Not right away, he said. We'd go back to America for a year, and only then come back to Israel for good.

My father had picked the wrong time to reveal his plans for the future. Much as I liked Israel, I didn't want to live there permanently. Maybe I was disappointed that the promised year's vacation was just a test. Why couldn't our parents have been straightforward about it? I was hurt.

Soon, however, my feelings changed radically. By the time we were ready to leave in the early summer of 1970, I no longer wanted to go along. I'd made friends, and they invited me to stay, at least until the end of the year. I asked for permission, but my parents were adamant. They had decided to return to the States, and I had to go with them.

I might have become a good Israeli had they let me stay. I was beginning to adjust. It wasn't fair for my parents to take me away. All those frequent moves, not only from city to city and country to country, but from one culture to another, was more than I could handle. One year Israel, one year America, and then again Israel—I couldn't cope with it. Moreover, when we returned to Israel we didn't go to Haifa but to Tel Aviv. Once more a new setting;

once more I had to start from scratch, to make new friends.

All my problems probably date back to the bitterness I felt then. Since age fourteen I have alternated between living in Israel and the United States, a wanderer between two worlds and two cultures who feels at home in neither.

I finished high school in Israel, but after I graduated, at age eighteen, I decided to leave without taking out Israeli citizenship. I returned to the States for a year and enrolled in college. But I didn't like it, and so I went back to Israel. I stayed for two years. I didn't know what to do with myself. I volunteered for the military, a desperate attempt to solve my identity problem, to convince myself that I was an Israeli. And what better way, I thought, than to do what Israelis do—join up. I am convinced that this, my second chance to acquire an Israeli identity, to become a part of Israeli society, would have worked. My parents had spoiled my first chance in 1970, when they forced me to leave with them. This time it was bureaucratic roadblocks. First they put me off for a year, then they lost my file, and when they finally set up a new one they put off my enlistment for yet another year. And when I thought that finally everything was straightened out, that I had reached my goal, they told me I was too old. And so all my efforts had been for naught.

Maybe I did everything wrong. Maybe my attitude was all wrong. Maybe I shouldn't have stormed into the draft office and said, "I've come to volunteer for work in the code department of navy intelligence." They looked at me and said, "So learn Hebrew." The reason they gave for turning down my application for enlistment was not knowing the language. I still have that rejection slip. But I'm convinced that language wasn't the real reason. I suspect that at the time they didn't need so many women. Most of the women back then were secretaries. Had I known that, I wouldn't have volunteered in the first place. Had they needed women they would have taken me. After all, they called up my younger brother, and his Hebrew was far worse than mine. As a matter of fact, he came back from the United States for his three-year army duty. It's not that he wanted to, but he was afraid that if he didn't he would never be allowed back in. And since our parents were living there he didn't want to take that risk.

After this setback there was nothing to keep me in Israel. I was still living with my parents. I didn't know what to do. But one thing was clear: I wasn't ready to move into my own apartment and furnish it. I was young and had no money. So once again I returned to the United States, and this time I stayed for ten years. Three years ago I came back here.

Actually the only reason I returned was Mother. Here's what happened. My parents had taken a year's sabbatical and come to the States, and during that time Father died. My mother was paralyzed; she didn't know what to do with herself. She had no friends in the States. Israel had become her home. She'd been living there since 1971, yet she was reluctant to return. Her three children were in the States and she was afraid of being alone. At the time of Father's death I wasn't doing anything particularly interesting, and my friends kept telling me that if I were to go to Israel I could probably persuade Mother to come along, and there she'd be able to put her life together again. So I packed up and went, and about eighteen months later Mother followed.

This time I returned because of Mother, but I'm sure the idea of Israel was a contributing factor. I'm sure I wouldn't have gone to Hungary if Mother were Hungarian. Of course I have emotional ties to Israel. I become aware of that whenever I'm abroad, but when I'm here I'm more conscious of my problems and dissatisfaction than of my affection and love for this country.

Even though I have become an Israeli citizen I still don't feel like an Israeli. However, that doesn't mean that I'm an American. I never was. I was never accepted as an American because of the way I spoke and because of my religion. Since my parents were European I spoke with an accent when I was little, and that didn't sound right to American ears. I was a foreigner, an almost-American. Americans tend to have a generation obsession. They talk about how many generations back their families go. A child of immigrants doesn't belong. I didn't fit into the place where I was born. Americans also have definite opinions about what people should be like, and those who don't live up to those expectations are excluded. That's why I never felt like an American.

Israel offered an alternative. Nobody there had any expectations of me. I was allowed to be myself. Of course, I have an American accent. I'll always have it. I can't hide it, and people here will always see me as an American. And for a long time I made a point of the American aspects of my personality. Perhaps it was my bitterness over having had to go back to the States with my parents that made me hold on to the American part of myself. In my dealings with Israelis I would always stress that I was an American. I'm not saying that I wasn't accepted as an Israeli. As a matter of fact, I think that Israelis like the idea of foreigners being Israelis. They may consider you an American, but at the same time they accept you as an Israeli, as one of theirs. It's hard to explain, but they never give you the feeling of not belonging. My Israeli friends—and I've always had Israeli friends—accept me just as I accept them. Whether Israeli or American doesn't matter. There are no barriers, nor am I conscious that this is a problem. On the contrary, it's when I'm with Americans that I become aware of it.

Will I stay in Israel for good? I don't know. It depends on how I feel when I get up in the morning. One day it's yes, the next, no. If I were to decide to return to the United States there aren't many places I'd want to live in. The one section I haven't tried and haven't learned to hate is the West. I like the desert, so I suppose I'd go to Arizona or New Mexico. But I'm not thinking of leaving here in the near future.

Naturally, one day I'd like to get married and have a family. Where would I want my children to grow up? Wherever I happen to be at the time, preferably Israel. But that depends on how things will go. It's hard to make a living here. At the moment I have a stupid job that's paid in dollars. I don't like it, but I had to take what I could get, to make enough to live on, and because of the language problem my options are limited. I hold Israel responsible for my present circumstances. I had a job I really enjoyed, with a newspaper, but because of conditions here now the paper folded.

There's no denying that my deficient command of Hebrew is a problem. I know kitchen Hebrew, but that's not enough for a decent job. True, I've spent almost half my life here and have heard Hebrew spoken, but I myself really never spoke it. And then there were long intervals when I was away from here. I didn't begin to speak Hebrew until three years ago when I came back. But I've never had the time to really learn the language. I had to look for a job when I came back. All I had in my pocket was a lousy 120 dollars. Things were very iffy. I had to make plans and organize my life, not ideal conditions for learning a new language. I didn't have any time. I didn't have time for lots of things.

My brothers managed their lives far better than I. As far as I know, they don't have any identity problem. My younger brother served in the Israeli army to make sure that he could return, and having served here, he began to feel a strong emotional tie to this country. He had originally intended to go to the States only long enough to finish college and then come back here. But that's not how things worked out. He decided that his prospects were better in the States, and he now lives in California. My older brother also is back in America, after having finished college here. He lives in Hollywood. He's the type, the kind of man who when he gets older will probably endow cultural projects in Israel. I don't think that either of my brothers have any emotional bonds to Israel.

As for me, I'll probably have to go on living with my inner conflicts, with the feeling of being an American in Israel and an Israeli in America. I've always dreamed of living in a place where I could say, "This is where I belong." Will it ever happen?

I don't know whether there exists a place where I'd be satisfied, though I'm not by nature a dissatisfied person. And I can't make either the United States or Israel responsible for my situation. I think there's something missing in this world, but that Israel is the better of the two countries. Why? Here I don't feel as dissatisfied when I wake up in the morning. Could it be the climate?

DAVID

I've been told lots of things in my life, but almost everything was wrong. You'll see, they used to say to me, by the time you grow up there won't be any more wars. Yet when I was eleven, my cousin was wounded in the battle of Jerusalem and came back with a big scar under his eye. It didn't exactly disfigure him, but I could never take my eyes off it. It made a deep impression on me when I was a child. I know it sounds crazy, but to this day I haven't been able to get rid of the idea that I too might come home scarred.

In November '73, a month after the beginning of the Yom Kippur War, I was called up. Shortly before, I had volunteered for work in a hospital. Every boy at the time just wanted to help, if not as a soldier then at least in a hospital. I was sent to the Rambam in Haifa, where I worked in the burn unit. It wasn't until much later, in Amsterdam, that I realized why I couldn't stand the smell of ham and eggs. That smell used to drive me out of my mind. It wasn't because ham was a forbidden food at home, and also not because it was fried, but because the mixture of eggs and meat smelled like human beings, like the burned soldiers in the tanks who were brought to the hospital. But in Amsterdam nobody understood me. The idea that a twenty-six-year-old was familiar with the smell of burned flesh seemed incomprehensible to people my age out for an evening's fun.

During my military service I was in a near-autistic state. I was a number—2205066—a body without a head. No feelings, no thoughts, just waiting for orders and obeying. When I entered the army I was still religious and wore a yarmulke. I wasn't sent to a combat unit; I was classified as a religious soldier on active duty. They put me into a unit for religious education. All I can remember is thousands of wasted hours. My most memorable activity was catching flies, a skill I had perfected. We were stationed in the Sinai Peninsula. Night patrol was the worst. The desert is cold and lonely, and I was afraid. Everything there is eerie, and that strange landscape bothered me. No other place is as eerie as the desert after dark. When two of us were on duty we at least could share our fear. But alone it was dreadful. Somehow I survived it, I no longer know how. When I was on night patrol I was often tempted to sound the alarm just to stir things up.

The army is an institution for very special types, for people who need structure, who're afraid of independence, who like things to be planned, including the place and time of their death. It is no place for people who want to grow and mature. Many who work for the military are simply afraid of normal life.

Our military talk of the "the country" as though it belongs to them, and that's exactly what they mean. I'm always annoyed when they talk of "the country." They say, "The country has the best fruit," or, "I'm going to the country." Nobody in France or Italy would ever talk like that. Here there still exists something like a "we" feeling. Everywhere, in the media, in school, always that collectivism. This constant pretense gets on my nerves.

The collectivist feeling emanates from the military, that male club that sticks together, inflated with their feelings of strength and bravery. More and more I tried to escape that stranglehold. My fear of total collectivization was greater than my craving for security. As a student I managed to avoid service for three years, but in the end they sent me to a training course for medics. It was a shock for me and I decided to do whatever I could to get thrown out. I made friends with another soldier, and the two of us decided to behave provocatively, hoping to get discharged. We bought two puppies and walked them on long leads throughout the camp.

Yet as so often in such situations one tends to underestimate the enemy and his skill in handling nonconformists. The two of us were invited for a talk, and were given twenty-four hours to decide which one of us was to be let go. The decision was to be ours alone. Only one could leave. They knew how to squelch our protest. I stayed, and things got worse. In yet another attempt to somehow get out I refused to accept my diploma at the end of the course. I maintained that I didn't know enough to make a good medic. The officer told me in that case they'd have to put me to the test. He kept his promise. I was soon given the opportunity to demonstrate my skills in the Lebanon war. Unfortunately, I'd been right. I really didn't know how to deal with injuries. I was completely at sea. The worst times were when the helicopters arrived with casualties and I was supposed to log them in. Standing in front of one such arrival who lay there without moving, I looked at him trying to figure out what was wrong with him. A doctor came over and hissed at me, "Not that one, he's long gone." That's when I realized he was dead.

During that war I thought I was going to lose my mind. The things that happened are not unusual in a war, but a person who is suddenly thrown into such a situation can lose his mind. Once we found ourselves in front of an Arab dwelling in south Lebanon. Our officer decided that that's where we'd bunk down. The soldiers went into the house to chase the family out. I tried to persuade the officer that we could just as easily settle down in the garden. Hopeless. At the time I was still religious and believed in fairness. I called the military chaplain and asked him to intervene, claiming that what we were doing violated the Bible, in particular the section dealing with war, but it did no good. The only thing I accomplished was to prevent the family from being chased off their land altogether.

Later, when the soldiers were showering in the garden, the man of the house asked me to tell the soldiers to stop parading around in the nude because there were young girls present. I was becoming something of a moral authority in our unit. Once I got up on a soap box, like in Hyde Park, and began to preach. I criticized various military acts, spoke of the moral responsibility of the army and similar issues. My sermon set off a spirited discussion. Suddenly nothing seemed so obvious anymore. Questions began to be asked: What is the military? What is the state? What are the rights of soldiers and civilians? What are we allowed to do as soldiers, and what are the limits?

We were so far from Israel, and nothing, not rules, not moral values, seemed terribly important any longer. The difference between the defense of our country and the invasion of a foreign land had become blurred.

When I returned I joined the peace movement and took part in demonstrations against the Lebanon campaign. And this rebellion against authority also precipitated my break with religion. I began to feel that all structures, not only the army, were oppressive, that all of them glorified the community and that the individual did not count. No personal dreams, no personal joys, no personal plans. Somebody does your thinking for you and you simply go along.

I was twenty-two when I stopped wearing a yarmulke. I ceased to be pious, stopped keeping the laws and eating kosher and observing the Sabbath. Taking off that head covering symbolized my rebellion against everything, not only against religious belief. It meant much more: my opposition to everything religion stood for—guilt feelings, the tragedy of the Jewish people from the Exodus to the Holocaust. For years I had been forced to remember tragedies, be it Masada or Amalek. Nothing but death and destruction. The common belief of a segment or an entire section of a city where the pious live also symbolized collective memory. It made no allowance for individual thinking, everything was prescribed, not by any one person but by sacred law. Those so inclined could demand total obedience by taking refuge in the Bible. And who would dare rebel against that? I often had the feeling that the army also exploits the submissiveness of the religious. In one way or another, all of us are influenced by our religion.

My first encounter with nonreligious people was in the army. Up to then I had lived in a ghetto of the pious. I didn't even know that there was such a thing as nonreligious people. My entire childhood and youth were focused on religion. I went to a boys' school where all contact with girls was taboo, but we also had no leisure time for play. We were in school all week long, and Saturdays were spent at the synagogue and with the family. The only nonreligious holiday was Independence Day. Then we could ride in cars, watch TV, and cook meals. Otherwise on Saturdays the only food we had was from a hot plate. Once every four years, on election day, we also had no school.

Life in our family, like in every pious family—and we weren't even all that Orthodox—was accompanied by constant guilt feelings. When I was twelve I went to a porno movie with some friends, a horrible sin. I lay awake all night waiting to see what would happen. When I found I was still alive next morning I thought to myself that perhaps not everything I'd been told was necessarily true. I began by taking very small dissenting steps, always waiting for punishment, and naturally was relieved when nothing happened.

Yet even now I still suffer from the aftereffects of my religious education. I am terribly naive and believe everything I'm told until the contrary is proved to me. My fantasies, even my language, are also different. When people raised in the religious tradition, completely uncritical as they are, begin to look at their surroundings with doubt, they tend to lose their bearings. When I read what is happening to the Arabs, Israel seems like a fascist state to me, as being anti-Semitic against Arabs and Oriental Jews, a racist society that calls conscientious objectors traitors and those who leave the country deserters.

I have a problem with the multiplicity of political parties and the contradictory statements of politicians. I was brought up to think that one either believes or disbelieves, that there's no in-between. But in modern society it is possible to believe a little more or a little less, or believe someone today and not believe him tomorrow. However, in that case, who is to believe in this country? Should my children grow up here? Or will Israel become a country without Jews because the handful of religious Jews will retreat into ghettos and in effect secede from the state?

In my parents' bedroom hangs a picture of a family. For a long time I didn't know it was a picture of my father's family that had perished in the Holocaust. My father had been in Dachau. He cut off one of his toes to get to the hospital, giving him a better chance to escape. He succeeded, but his scar still bothers him. Every day he applies an antibiotic ointment to the spot where his toe once was. It's the family miracle cure. The first time I went abroad by myself I had to take some along. When we were little, as another reminder of past suffering, we weren't allowed to move our beds against the wall for fear of the cold. The wall, Father always told us, stored up the cold.

My parents were pained by my turning away from religion. They had always looked on me as their charming son, a little wild, a good student, the hope of the family. And then came this step, so different from my brothers. But there was nothing I could do, I had to break away.

Today if I were asked to define the meaning of Israel I wouldn't know what to say. As an Israeli I feel that an opportunity has been missed, that things could be much better, without having an answer. However, I know what I personally miss: a feeling of security and tranquillity. Every Arab workman, every newscast, every letter from the government makes me uneasy. My rejection of religion has brought me a great deal of freedom but also a great deal of insecurity. It is difficult to grow up in a cage and suddenly have to fly, even though you know you have wings.

ILONA

Until 1974 I lived in Czernowitz, in the Soviet Union. We knew that there was an Israel and that we had relatives there. Apart from that, however, that country meant nothing to us. Emigration? Out of the question. Father wouldn't hear of it. We couldn't even talk about it at home. He was an assimilated Jew, a Communist, and a much-decorated Red Army officer in the Second World War. He felt himself part and parcel of the upper layer of Czernowitz society, and as a physician he was consulted by the local elite—artists, politicians, actors, and writers. They all came to him, which is probably why discrimination never became much of an issue with us. Like the majority of Jews we were naive. Of course we knew that there was anti-Semitism, and we even had some firsthand experience, but we thought that with our connections we'd never have any serious problems. We were to find out.

My first personal experience came at school. Even though I was a very good student, my math grade was lowered to keep me from winning top honors. My math teacher visited us at home to tell us about it beforehand. Embarrassed yet candid, she confessed that she'd had to change my grade because I was Jewish. I was miserable and angry, and I felt utterly helpless. I tried to tell myself that it was just something I'd have to learn to live with. My father, who had always defended the system, was furious and refused to accept it. He said that I shouldn't take it lying down, that I should demand a review. But I knew that even if they revised my math grade they'd just change my grades in other subjects. I was Jewish, and therefore I wasn't going to be allowed to win top honors, even if no one would ever admit to the reason: my Jewishness. I tried to shrug it off, joking that I supposed the prize would go to whoever had copied from me. I was becoming well-versed in the Russian habit of keeping one's mouth shut, of not speaking up, out of fear that it would only make matters worse.

The upshot was that despite my excellent grades I didn't get admitted to medical school for another two years. There was a Jewish quota. They must have been afraid of too many educated Jews. Since most Jewish students opted for medicine, the medical school had the highest number of Jewish applicants. Many went to Siberia, where getting into medical school was still easier, but I refused to give up, and after a two-year wait I was admitted in Czernowitz. I didn't encounter any overt anti-Semitism at school. Nobody ever called me dirty Jew or any other derogatory name, but it was always there, like a part of the landscape of the indigenous culture.

Many of the Jewish families lived very isolated lives. We were among the exceptions. And Jews also didn't date non-Jews. When one of my closest friends, not Jewish, started dating a Jewish boy, her parents decided to move the family to another city. Whenever she came to our house, my old grandmother would say to me in Yiddish, "Don't you have any other girlfriends?"

That tension was always there, and as time went on my life became more and more difficult. Once, on a visit to a neurological clinic, we saw a patient who crowed like a cock, never saying a word. But when I walked past him— I look Jewish—he began to scream that all Jews should be killed. The last smidgen of brain power left to him was hatred of Jews.

I've never experienced a pogrom. No one has ever tried to kill me. Yet I always knew fear. Because I knew what had happened here in the past, I was afraid when I passed people coming out of church. On Christian holidays I tried to steer clear of churches and processions. Over the years my fear increased.

Ironically, it was my father who first broached the subject of emigration. The end of the sixties saw the first big wave of emigration. Our acquaintances kept on talking about it, and more and more of them left. A joke was then making the rounds: Two Jews are talking to each other and a third one joins them. "I don't know what you're talking about," he says to them, "but I'm also thinking of going to Israel."

We applied for emigration permits, and that's when our troubles started. To begin with, I was asked for an official statement from the university that they were aware of my intention to leave; Father was asked for a similar statement from his place of employment. Both these requests were tantamount to immediate ouster. I had to leave school, and Father had to resign. However, in Russia people who don't work are subject to arrest. With one stroke we had become outlaws.

For eighteen months we sat at home waiting for permission to leave. During that period I was ordered to appear at the university. I found myself in a lecture hall crowded with students, about five hundred of them. Very politely I was invited to step up on the platform. Standing there in front of all those students, I was asked to explain why I was betraying my country by wanting to leave. The Jews were not the target of criticism, they said. Israel was. That was their euphemism for anti-Semitism. Yet many of my fellow students were genuinely upset over my decision. They came from all over the country—Russians, Ukrainians, Moldavians, and what have you—and they tried to convince me that I was making a grave mistake. I pleaded helplessness, saying that it was my family's decision, not mine.

The pressure on us was relentless. My sister's family was refused permission to leave because my brother-in-law allegedly was the possessor of official secrets. He'd been nothing more than a laborer at an army post, a job he'd left five years earlier. Besides, the only work he'd done there was dig ditches.

The government offered to return us to our positions if we'd agree to withdraw our applications. But all we wanted to do was just get out. During those difficult months the friendship extended to us by an old friend of Father's meant a great deal. In the early 1950s my father had worked as a physician in a small village. He and the local priest, the only educated people there, became friends. At one point the priest fell seriously ill and Father saved his life. Now that my father wasn't working and we had nothing to live on, the priest's wife secretly left food for us at our doorstep. Those two people had very little themselves, but neither did they have fear.

Finally we were able to leave. We took a train to Prague, and from there to Vienna. I will never forget the strange scene at the station when we left. All our acquaintances, friends, and relatives came to see us off, but nobody said a word. They were all afraid. We'd walk by them, they'd

look away if we tried to make eye contact, and only look
up once we had passed them. About fifty people from the
village where my father had worked and helped so many
also showed up. They stood there silently, some in tears.
Yet no one said a word, no good-byes, no embraces,
nothing.

I've now been living here in Israel for the past fifteen
years and am not in touch with my old home. Even though
I spent the greater part of my life in Russia, the major
portion of my conscious, independent existence has been
here in Israel. My memories of Czernowitz are impersonal
images—houses, streets, posters—but except for a select
few, perhaps a neighbor or an occasional student, and the
police and officials, no people. I know I didn't go through
what Jews went through in the past, but if I sit here among
other Jews watching TV broadcasts from Moscow, I find
I'm not really interested.

My place is here in Israel. This is where I've studied, this
is where I've married, this is where my children were born.
I don't hate the past, nor do I hate the Russians, not even
those who treated us so shabbily. But everything is so far
away. It no longer means anything. My husband would
like to visit there and take a look, but I don't want to. My
sister has remained completely Russian. She looks at Russian TV, invites only Russians to her parties, and speaks
Russian at home. I'm glad to have gotten away from all
that. I took to life here like a fish to water, but neither my
sister nor my mother ever adjusted. They're sorry they
came. My husband is an Israeli and so integration was
probably easier for me. Because he didn't like it when I
spoke Russian with my family in his presence I gradually
began to change my language as well as many of my habits.
Now I actually prefer reading books in Hebrew even
though lots of Russian books and publications are available

here. But they don't interest me. And when I do read them I find them strange. It's like going through boxes of old photos over and over again.

Many Russians living here are so angry at the past that they support the rightist parties, including Kahane's. To them every progressive party is like the Communists. And Likud has cleverly exploited those feelings. Jerusalem is sacred to most of the Russians. When it comes to the question of returning the territories or to the conflict with the Palestinians, these Russians are among the most extreme. Even though they themselves once were the victims of oppression, they have little compassion for others.

I'm not particularly interested in the political parties, nor do I see any big difference between the two major ones. I'm also annoyed by the simplistic equation "Orientals, Likud; Ashkenazim, Labor." In the Diaspora the Jews are always the smart ones, but here in their own country one sees very little of their vaunted intelligence.

If I were asked to say what, after fifteen years, being an Israeli means to me, I'd have to say identifying with suffering, taking pleasure in what I've achieved, however minor, not constantly complaining or being dissatisfied or refusing to change.

And I never want to leave here. Israel is a miracle. The country is like an adolescent girl. I hope they let it grow to maturity.

ZIPPORAH

I am a prize exhibit of the lasting impact of the Holocaust.
Everything my parents experienced and failed to come to
terms with has been handed down to me, and via me also
to my children. And don't think for a moment that I'm the
only one here like this. I feel intuitively that many of our
actions, political as well as personal, are reactions to the
madness of the Second World War. Yet we're told we
mustn't look at things in this light.

I was born in Tel Aviv in 1950. My parents came from
Poland. They had survived the Holocaust. How? I don't
know. Shortly after the war they arrived here with the
Youth Aliyah. Both were the only members of their re-
spective families to have survived. All the rest were exterminated in Auschwitz. That's all I know. Nothing about
my grandparents or any other relatives, and nothing about
how my parents survived. Neither of them has ever spoken
about it. Life before 1946 does not exist for them. A brave
effort, but they've paid for it by dramatically reliving everything they refuse to talk about or remember. Perhaps they
only wanted to protect me, but the result was the exact
opposite.

My father suffered nightmares; he'd scream for help, toss about, and cry. Always the same. I'd wake up and hear everything. My mother would get up and try to calm him down, give him a tranquilizer, and tell him to take a walk. That helped, and he'd be able to go back to sleep. Mother used to be Father's stable support. Later all that changed.

When I was little these scenes naturally frightened me. Mother would explain that Father'd had a troubled childhood and was still haunted by it. Be glad, she'd say, that you have it so good, and don't ask any more questions. That's all. No explanation of what really had happened. Yet on the other hand, they couldn't hide the fact that I had no living relatives. I knew instinctively that something terrible must have happened long before I was born. The reason I had no grandparents or aunts or uncles or cousins, Mother used to tell me, was that they had to stay with the Germans. The Germans were bad people and I should be happy to be far away from them. I must never believe that they had changed, whatever anyone should try to tell me. Evil people remain evil, and evil nations as well. These are facts, and there's nothing to be done about it. Thus evil was a constant presence in our lives, and Germany—all Germans and everything German—was evil incarnate. But it wasn't until I went to school that I heard the name Hitler or the word Holocaust.

Most of our friends and neighbors were also Holocaust survivors. I didn't think that there was anything peculiar about them. Everyone we knew had nightmares, woke up screaming, and cried for no apparent reason. But it was an iron law in Israel not to hark back to the past, to think only of the future. Of course there were public commemorations, an endless stream of commemorations. In school we soon learned everything about the Holocaust. What we were remembering and mourning were the dead. Nobody gave a thought to the damage being inflicted on the living. The survivors had better things to do than bemoan and suffer over the past. Now the task was to build. A new country was to come into being, a land for the Jews.

There was nothing wrong with this except for the inevitable delayed reaction to the Holocaust, namely parental overprotectiveness. I was an only child, as were many of my friends. Today I know that the fear-ridden watchfulness of our parents was the product of their traumatic past. Many ordinarily routine situations took on an air of catastrophe.

It began with eating. If, God forbid, I occasionally had no appetite, the world threatened to come to an end. My mother would fall into a near-depression. I was always dressed too warmly lest I catch cold. Until the age of eleven or so I was not allowed to walk to school by myself even though my school was just across the street. Mother always took me and called for me, as did many other mothers of daughters. When I began to fight against this protectiveness, Mother would stand at the window and watch me cross the street, and she'd sit at the window watching me when I played in the yard with my friends. She panicked when I was out of sight. Every step away from her turned into a battle. The perfectly normal developmental steps in the mother-child relationship made her literally sick. My maturing became her ruin. Everything that gave me pleasure gave her pain. But having found out in school what she had gone through I, like many others in my shoes, had a problem about fighting for my independence. The Holocaust hung like a sword over my needs.

When I began to go out with my friends there were always emotional scenes before I left the house and when I got back. Fear prevented Mother from behaving rationally, and all my efforts to calm her were useless. Father showed far greater understanding for my mother's fears than for my needs, and he invariably took her part. None of this took the form of great dramatic clashes. I was far too cowed for that. No wonder, given my upbringing. Yet I did not want to give in to this to me unreasonable panic. Like other girls of my age I wanted to go to the movies, to ice cream parlors, to parties. And I did.

And then came the day when I was to join the army. Our household went into mourning. Mother looked as though she was about to collapse; still I managed to tear myself away and leave. Only much later did I learn from a neighbor that once I was gone Mother broke down and spent two weeks in a psychiatric clinic. She has since become a regular visitor there. Every leave-taking ends in catastrophe, particularly for my father, because he then has to look after Mother. Things are getting progressively worse. My military service was like a final farewell from which she never recovered. I now live in a kibbutz, a three-hour drive from my parents' place, really not very far were it not for those parting scenes. I, for my part, solve the problem by not visiting home very often. I have the feeling that in a way Father doesn't mind too much. He finds it easier to cope with Mother's depressive states than with the tragic farewell scenes.

Over the years Mother's fearfulness has gotten worse and worse. Her depressions make life difficult. However, it is not only pain that's killing her, but hatred as well. She cannot find any peace. Somewhere in the world evil is always lurking, and it won't ever go away. Not until I was an adult did I find out that all the other Holocaust victims were getting restitution payments. Not my parents, because Mother said she didn't want to take any dirty German money. I went behind her back, and I finally got Father to accept a pension from Germany. Father was a music teacher; Mother stayed at home. Teachers here aren't paid all that well, and the little Father made from private lessons he spent on violin lessons for me. It was the kind of thing proper young Ashkenazi girls did, particularly daughters of music teachers. The pension he receives here is quite small, and so the money from Germany allows him to live halfway decently.

I've been living in the kibbutz for fifteen years. My husband was born here. We have two children. Actually it's sad to see how life repeats itself. My children hardly know their grandparents. Father has visited us at most twice, and Mother never, and all because of those good-bye scenes. And because of Mother's sad condition I can't take my children along on those rare occasions when I go home for a visit. The funereal atmosphere in that house is not suitable for young children. Windows and blinds are hardly ever opened there. Mother spends most of her days in this dark apartment in bed. The apartment is also a little messy. She keeps on getting up to look for some old photos or papers in chests and drawers in a desperate search for God knows what. When she finds what she wanted she leaves the house looking as though a hurricane had swept through it. Then she crawls back into bed. Father tries to keep order, but it's impossible. She goes through this routine almost daily.

I feel that we ought to find a decent place for Mother and have Father move in with us. At least let him live out his life in peace. The kibbutz is an ideal place for children and older people. Everything here is green and friendly. There'd be people his age here, and he'd probably also be able to find some fellow musicians. But he won't hear of it. He says he owes it to Mother to take care of her as long as he's able to. She deserves it, he says. In a way I admire his commitment. I can't bear to spend even ten minutes with her. On the other hand, I feel that he deserves something better after all he's been through; she's beyond help anyway.

The situation between my parents and myself is typical for the difference between our two generations. For years we kept on asking how the generation of the Holocaust victims could have gone to death so unresistingly. Many of us cannot accept it, even though there's been an effort to publicize the fight against the Germans. Still, the way they bore their suffering in silence is typical for that generation. As it turns out, however, their silent suffering hasn't been all that silent. Many of my generation have been damaged by either overprotectiveness or the relentless pressure to show strength.

I suppose I can be said to be completely Israelized. I, too, can't understand sheeplike acquiescence. I fight back. I won't just take it. Almost all the parents of people my age are immigrants, men and women who somehow managed to survive. This collection of refugees quickly found a new identity and gained national pride. True, almost all of us are children of victims and of persecution, and it hasn't been all that simple to slough off the feelings of our parents. But most of us managed to. Thank God, today we're no longer victims.

Even so, my life here in the kibbutz also is a flight from my parents. But of course mine can't be called a typical parental home. In a home situation as twisted as mine escape isn't necessarily a negative move. On the contrary. Rather than fall into depression and self-pity, I have made the best out of a bad situation by looking for and finding a substitute family: the kibbutz.

It's possible that I might not be able to live in the city on my own. There are all those fears going back to my childhood. Here in the manageable setting of kibbutz life I can cope with them more easily. I am consumed by fears.

I, too, am an overprotective mother. My mother's influence is not to be denied, even though I try to fight it. I am trying to become more stable.

I'm not angry at Mother for having been what she was and still is. How could I? It wasn't her fault. Of course the Germans are responsible. But I do blame her for not having done anything about her problems, for accepting and suffering under them as she suffered under the Nazis. And by not trying to help herself she has handed on her pain to the next generation.

I also no longer blame the Germans. Nor would it help to settle the question of guilt. That is yet another difference between me and my parents. They sit around and bewail what has happened to them, holding the Nazis responsible for everything. But I'm not looking for guilt, let alone for the guilty. What's the good of it today? Still, I've never been to Germany or Austria. I have no desire to go there. When I got out of the army my husband and I took a trip to Europe. My husband wanted to go to the Alps; he'd heard that Austria was cheaper than Switzerland. But I wasn't ready to go to Austria, and certainly not to Germany. As far as I'm concerned the people there are monsters. That's a childhood impression I can't shake off. Perhaps one day I'll have the strength to overcome this prejudice. For the time being, however, it's not an important enough issue for me. I still have plenty of other demons to deal with. As to Germany, laying that specter to rest can wait.

SAMI

I was born in Tel Hasnomer, a renowned hospital at Givatym, near Tel Aviv. When I was twelve we moved to another suburb, Zahala, where my mother's parents lived in a beautiful house. My parents simply built another story on to it. My grandparents had come here from Bulgaria a long time ago. Mother was born in Israel. My parents felt uneasy about having Mother's aging parents live alone, and so they hit on the idea of expanding the house.

My father's parents are from Poland, or more exactly, my grandfather is; Grandmother comes from Germany. They spent the war years in Switzerland, and that's where my father was born and grew up. As an enthusiastic, idealistic member of Shomer Hazair, a Zionist youth group, he dreamed of one day going to Israel, and when he was seventeen he did. As soon as he arrived in Israel he joined a kibbutz. It was the life he'd always envisioned.

When my mother's parents came to Israel they joined a left-wing kibbutz, but they left it when Mother was born. My grandmother couldn't stand the idea of having her child grow up in a children's house. She is and has always been a very caring person, very maternal and warm. So my grandparents left the kibbutz and moved to a Bulgarian section of Tel Aviv. I don't even know whether it still exists.

Grandfather worked for the military, and when the settlement in Zahala was founded army families were given housing there. By the time I came to Zahala many of the people living there were retirees. That's all changed. In the last ten years a number of well-to-do young families have moved in. But when I grew up there I was surrounded by old people, with only a few children from other settlements.

The move to Zahala wasn't very good for me. Almost all the children at my school came from rich homes and were very different from me. And I wasn't a very good student back then. The children and the adults were all very snobbish, and I didn't like it a bit. And the children were always fighting among themselves over who could be admitted into their group and who couldn't. Newcomers were despised and ignored, while at Givatym newcomers were almost squeezed to death with love. I still remember a boy who had a great problem making friends. His mother brought him to school every day, and he'd cry when she left. So we decided to have a party and invite him. That evening we got everything ready, but he didn't show up. We went to his house and almost dragged him off with us to the party. Once there he became very friendly. Here everything was different. At their first party they didn't want to let me in. They said I wasn't invited. That's the difference between poor and rich. I suppose it's the same everywhere. Even now I have hardly any friends here.

Still, it was a fairly new settlement, not as built up as today, and there was lots of open space. I hunted snakes and cats and birds and roamed through the fields and plantations. The organized Boy Scouts didn't interest me, but my parents wanted me to join that overstuffed, rich crowd, and so I did.

Once we went on night maneuvers in an orange plantation. It was pitch-black, and they ordered me to bring up the rear. Suddenly three boys waylaid me, pulled me into the bushes, and beat me up. One of them stepped on my belly and another one peed on me. I didn't scream and I didn't cry. I think that made them even angrier. I never again went back there, and I have never forgotten it either. Most of those boys went directly from the Scouts to the Nahal. [Nahal is the acronym for a paramilitary youth organization offering intensive training and supporting the establishment of settlements.]

I was called up to the army right after graduating from high school, but it was found that I wasn't a hundred percent physically fit. They'd discovered blood in my urine, and so I had only sixty-five points. The military is very particular. Actually I felt quite fit, but they assigned me to clerical duties. Later I was reexamined, and suddenly I had ninety-seven points, almost the maximum. In a way I was happy about this. Even though as an office worker my life was easier, I still couldn't stand it. I had nothing to do in this office. It was boring and I didn't feel motivated. I'd never thought military service would be fun, but still I wanted to do something useful. It's no pleasure to feel that suddenly you're worthless, completely superfluous, sitting at a desk with nothing to do.

When you first get into the army they don't make you feel that you're important. In fact, they make you feel very small. And above all you've got to obey. After all, you're a nothing. It's the same sort of discipline as in school. But the consequences aren't the same, and that's something you've got to learn. I'd never expected that I could do what I want in the army, but on the other hand I certainly never expected that kind of pressure.

They didn't take my needs into account. Having been

classified for limited service, I sat at a desk compiling lists
and shuffling paper. And because I was good at my job
they refused to transfer me. I filed a complaint and was
told I'd be assigned to the medics. That suited me fine, but
it resulted in a battle between the office and the medical
corps. It took five months, but ultimately I got my transfer.
This change was very good for me. I wanted to become
a real soldier. Unless you're a soldier you're nothing in this
country. I was motivated and proud, and completely exhausted from the training. The course lasted four months.
From morning to night nothing but relentless pressure. But
the things I was learning there really interested me and
weren't limited to purely military matters.

After the Lebanon war the mood in the country was very
depressed. No one was enthusiastic about going into the
army. That's when I was drafted. A lot of my friends advised me to do as little as possible. Both my grandfather
and father had been in the army, but it was at a time when
the very existence of the country was at stake. Surrounded
by enemies, they were fighting for survival. The Lebanon
war wasn't seen the same way. Many felt it was an un-
necessary war. We suddenly were discovering aggressive
attitudes toward our neighbors, and that was something
new. The issue wasn't whether that foreign land was harboring terrorists; rather, we had invaded a neighboring
country and were acting as policemen. That violated what
I'd been taught and my vision of our state.

Yet on the other hand I also didn't want to run away.
After all, this is where I was born, and that entails obli-
gations. Had I been born in Australia I might not feel this
way. That's why you can always hear good advice from
abroad, but here things are different. All of us have been
damaged by the decades-old conflicts. Where else in the
world can you find this special tie to the military? Israel

has been in existence for forty years, and every ten years has seen a war. That is bound to affect the public psyche. If there won't be peace soon I think we'll gradually become stupefied.

In the army I was never afraid of dying, but I was forever afraid that one of my friends might fail to come back from a mission. Fear made us cynical. You try to deny it and crack jokes about the terrible things that are happening. On Saturdays when I was home on leave I'd spend hours telephoning my friends, and I was happy when I reached all of them. Since the intifada I haven't been called up. Even if I were I wouldn't be sent to the territories because after I finished my medic's training course I became an instructor. I was offered a commission to stay in the army, but I turned it down.

If they were to call me today I'd try to join a combat outfit. I would also behave very differently than before. When I was in training there were constant political discussions about the military. We kept on talking about whether it was right to go along, whether the order to march into Lebanon was justified or morally legitimate. But a soldier who asks such questions can't fight. It is almost as though thinking and fighting were mutually exclusive. Now I draw a strict line between politics and the military. Politically I suppose I'm on the left, but I don't think it's right to refuse service in the territories. Where are the limits of my moral claims? That's a question which probably occupies every young Israeli nowadays, because every one of us may find himself in a situation tomorrow in which he must fire at children in order to save his own life. Yet I fear anarchy more than I do a rigid military that does not tolerate dissent.

One of my friends recently served in the territories. He kept on talking about his inner conflict. During the day, he said, you join in everything—beatings, shooting, driving women out of houses about to be blown up—and you have no problem with any of it. You're ready to maim the first stone-thrower you come across without a qualm. But later, back at home, you feel miserable thinking about it, and toss about in bed unable to sleep. But while it's happening you feel nothing. There you stand as a soldier with your moral claims, surrounded by hundreds spitting at you, calling you names, throwing bottles and stones, calling your mother a whore. And as you walk through a village, and out of every window somebody is shouting, you begin to be afraid. An incredible fear takes hold of you, and then comes the moment when you can't stand it any longer and you hit out at the next person you see. For a fleeting moment you simply have to feel that you're still stronger and able to defend yourself or you'll go crazy. Most of us, he told me, then just hit out, without looking, and you see these terrible explosions of rage. In the evening or on weekends they sit around and talk about what's happened. Feeling desperate, they must keep talking. He himself, he said, had talked about it so often, and almost everyone he knows feels tormented.

When I was discharged from the army after three years it wasn't all that easy to start over again as a civilian. You experience something like separation trauma. For three years you had the feeling of having been important and needed, and suddenly it's all over; you're suspended like a tiny particle in the atmosphere, without support and purpose. I was simply afraid. What should I do now, where should I work and live? In the army you are taken care of; there are no existential worries. This cocoon gives rise to almost childish fantasies. We dreamed of sudden wealth and of the traveling we'd do after getting out: South America, Asia, North America. I was going to see the world.

But when I took off my uniform I was afraid to look for a job or an apartment.

My then girlfriend and I made grandiose plans. In our imagination we saw ourselves traveling around the world. She still had eighteen months of military service, and so we decided to wait. I waited and waited, and we talked and talked, and then, when the time came, we broke up. I'd had a little time to think, and our imaginary trips made it possible for me to deal with the freedom trauma of civilian life. Slowly I found my way back to everyday life, able to become absorbed into another system. I applied to Mogen David Adom, the Israeli Red Cross, and in view of my military training they hired me on the spot. I taught, and also cared for patients. For three months I looked after a disabled soldier. I became his friend, his mother, his father, his psychologist, everything.

I was also faced with the problem that after having been away for three years I was once more living at home. There were constant fights. I wanted to move, but I was saving for my never-to-be trip with my girlfriend. So, dissatisfied as I was, I stayed at home, making life difficult for my parents.

My work with my disabled veteran began to take up more and more of my time. At first I had to fight my guilt feelings. After all, the only thing I'd done was train other medics. And I landed in this cushy spot because of a possibly erroneous blood test. If not for that I might be the one lying here, unable to move. Then I tried to tell myself that because of what I had done many other medics may have saved lives. But however hard I tried to come to terms with this issue, I couldn't really convince myself.

My wounded veteran had suffered extensive brain damage. He was paralyzed on one side of his body and suffered from seizures and memory loss. His life was effectively over. The pills he took against the seizures made him woozy and sleepy. He also had lost the use of his hands. I began to identify with him more and more, living his life, until I had to quit the job. After being with him for three months I was in terrible shape. I slept next to him, always afraid that he might have a seizure. When that happened it was like death staring me in the face. When he felt good we would talk for hours, about his injury, about death, about his future. After he was wounded he lay in a coma for three days, and then he spent months in various hospitals and rehabilitation centers. Again and again he would talk about the first time, after having spent months in bed, he managed to crawl out and slowly drag himself over to the window. He wanted to jump out but couldn't pull himself up. Two years later he was able to walk with a cane, even drive a car, although he keeps dozing off. I'm convinced that one day he'll have a fatal accident. His daily routine never varies. He really doesn't know what day of the week it is.

I suddenly found I couldn't go on. It was all too much for me. When I told him that I wouldn't be coming anymore he became angry and sad, as though his girlfriend told him she was leaving. His mother was dead and his father didn't know how to cope with this situation. Now a friend of mine is looking after him, and I'm glad.

That's what Jewish daily life looks like. Either you yourself are killed in action or a friend dies or is seriously wounded and you're called on to help. People here say that if someone in the New York subway drops dead nobody pays any attention. In Israel it's an entirely different matter. Here everybody behaves as though it's one big family. Often it becomes too much. If a headlight of your car is out everybody will comment on it. People are constantly mixing into your life with good advice.

I'm like all the other Israelis. I keep on complaining and criticizing, yet I'd never want to leave. My grandparents experienced the worst excesses of hatred of Jews and came here to live among their own. Today they and my parents are proud Israelis. My father's sister considers herself a Swiss. She doesn't feel like a Jew and most certainly doesn't want to come here. All this in a single family! What a difference education makes.

When I left the Red Cross I applied to the police. There I did the same thing I'd done in the army: teach first aid. Then I began to study zoology. Now my life is slowly beginning to take shape. I have some income from my police job, and it also exempts me from reserve duty. I would like to become a veterinary, start a family, have children and my own apartment. Somehow I feel more positive about life. The aftereffects of my army days have worn off. I feel that I've lost a lot of time: the training, the three years in the service, and the problems afterward. If peace should ever come here—you can't imagine how much we Israelis would be spared.

MIRIAM

The street in Tel Aviv where I spent my early years now is full of cars, day and night. When I was born it was still a quiet street of small houses and gardens, but it slowly began to change. The small houses were razed and the sort of rental buildings that you see all over Tel Aviv began to go up. My parents were given an apartment in one of these buildings. The old green islands are gone. Instead, we now have an expanse of gray, lightless buildings. But I still remember what it looked like before. Perhaps it wasn't all that idyllic, not what you imagine small houses and gardens to be like, and I didn't appreciate their real beauty until much later. Many families with young children used to live there, and the grown-ups and children were in constant contact with one another. Even when traffic became heavier we could still play outdoors, and later on in the courtyards. The neighborhood didn't have the character of a city; it was more like a small town. Now it's different. I don't live there anymore, but I visit, and when I look at the buildings I think that everything used to be more beautiful. Maybe one always feels like that.

We are not newcomers. Both my parents are native-born

Israelis. One member of the previous generation, my father's mother, was even born here, I think in Tel Aviv. A long time ago her family fled in the opposite direction. They went from Israel to Egypt in the First World War when the Turks threatened the Jewish population. Later my grandmother returned to Tel Aviv.

My mother's mother came from Bulgaria to Israel to study, and she stayed on, in Tel Aviv. Her parents remained in Bulgaria. She met Grandfather, who'd come here from Poland, in school. I think he was teaching Hebrew. That's how they met, and some years later they married. Mother was born in Tel Aviv. So was Father. One might say we are the third generation living in Tel Aviv.

All the children I went to school with were native Israelis. I don't remember any immigrant children. At school we never had the feeling of being among strangers. All the children came from the same neighborhood. All the people who lived here were old Israelis; no strangers ever settled there. We wore school uniforms, light-blue rayon skirts or blue pants, and in the summer we wore hats to protect us against the sun. And in class we had to sit with folded hands.

After a long period of calm, war broke out in 1967. I remember it graphically—the air-raid sirens sometimes went off as we were coming home from school. We were told that if that happened we were to go to the nearest shelter, or if we saw planes, to take cover in a ditch. I can still see it all. Once the sirens went off while we were in class.

My father was in the army when the war broke out. The hill where he was stationed was attacked, and I remember locking myself in the bathroom and crying. I was so afraid. I promised to be very good, even to eat butter, which I didn't like at all. I was very skinny, and Mother was forever after me to eat buttered bread. I resolved to do everything she asked so that nothing would happen to Father, and also to keep her happy. I was nine at the time.

Father survived the war. His unit was stationed in Jericho. We visited him and his brother. I remember the winding road leading up the hill. There were burned-out army vehicles everywhere, and tanks. It was shortly before the end of the war. In Jericho everything was so strange, so different, with red flowers, peaceful, like a tropical island. Quite a contrast to the highway with its broken-down vehicles.

I also remember that everything seemed absolutely logical. I felt like a visitor. To this day a chill runs down my spine when I think of it, but then everything looked completely normal. Nobody here was an intruder or a victor. Of course, I was still very young, but that's how I felt then, and even afterward. I liked to take walks in the West Bank, through the old city of Jerusalem and Bethlehem. It was exotic and very lovely, all those shop windows with their strange Oriental wares. As I told you, I remember a feeling of belonging. Not anymore, maybe because of my political views. Now when I go there I feel like a stranger, someone who has no right to walk around there. And so, for reasons of ideology, I stay away. I feel uneasy about going to the West Bank.

I suppose it all began with the Yom Kippur War. I spent almost three years in the army. The first two I was in charge of the basic training of young girls. After that I attended an officers' training school, and I also continued to teach. At one time I was assigned to a special training program for girls from underprivileged families. After that I also taught reading and writing as part of the course, and in addition I helped out in hospitals. When I was in the army, three years after the Yom Kippur War, the country wasn't at war, but the events of the preceding years had left their mark on me.

I was still in high school when the war broke out. Many of my friends volunteered for hospital duty, and so did I. A cousin and I went to the hospital. It was fun. We were taken from ward to ward. The place was full of volunteers. The last stop was the plastic surgery ward. I turned to my cousin, puzzled over what on earth this was supposed to mean. What did this have to do with war? But our help was badly needed. Minutes later I saw my first casualty, and I suddenly realized where I was. Almost all the wounded, especially all burn victims, ended up in this ward.

I think I just turned off. It was dreadful. I remember the smell of burnt flesh, of nurses crying and vomiting, but I just withdrew into a shell and did what I was told. I was still very young, but I functioned. I stayed for quite some time. Once everything was over I began to reflect on what I had seen. As far as I'm concerned there is no such thing as a just war. But, being an Israeli, I saw army service as a logical stage, a part of myself. It would never have occurred to me to question it. On the contrary, I wanted to give it my all, and I stayed longer than the two mandated years.

I couldn't tell you what my choice would be today. Of course age is an important factor. In the United States and Europe young people can get deferments and join the army later. And women are exempted altogether. Once you're older your attitude changes. You're bound to be more apprehensive, more careful, to weigh the consequences of your acts. When I was eighteen everything looked very different. I'd just finished school, and all of us wanted to belong, to participate.

Today's youth is both more cynical and more ideological. In my time it was different. I'm sure all this is connected with the intifada. Most young people of course go into the army, but they're not as naive as we. Some don't want to pay the price for an ideology not of their own making, and others don't want to serve in the occupied territories. Who in my day would have given a thought to whether what we as soldiers were doing was just? Not a single one. Out of the question. Israel, a state our parents had built with their own hands and sweat, had to be safeguarded. We, the young, had to give of ourselves to protect it. The idea that an Israeli soldier might one day be indicted for an act of brutality was simply inconceivable.

After the war I studied psychology for six years. I got my B.A. in general psychology and an M.A. in clinical psychology. After that I began to practice Gestalt therapy, and that's what I am doing now.

My husband served in the army during the Lebanon war as an officer in a tank unit. When he was first called up he served in the Golan Heights. Things were still undecided; Syria had not yet taken a clear position. Only later were the lines more clearly drawn. We came to the conclusion that it was not right to embark on this war, but nevertheless he stayed in the army. But when he was called up in the reserves after the war, his unit was sent to Lebanon and he refused. Those were hard times. He served out his army term in prison.

I thank God that neither my friends nor my family were critical of our decision. They helped me out. Most of them now agree with me and my husband. We don't want any more wars. Nothing can motivate us to put on a uniform and shoot at other human beings. When my husband was in prison I hadn't yet completed my studies, and I was also expecting our first baby. When I visited him in prison I felt like a character in a movie, that none of this was happening to me. He was behind bars and we weren't allowed to talk.

An absurd, sad situation. I felt as though I was stepping out of my body and looking at us on the screen.

The people I came into contact with regularly knew about our situation. It was wearing, because they all wanted to talk about it, and they all had an opinion. Some disagreed with me and said one shouldn't think about it so much but simply serve one's term like an eighteen-year-old. Those weren't ideological arguments. Rather, these people criticized my husband for leaving his friends, who were putting their lives on the line, in the lurch, while he himself was safe. Why should others risk their lives for the rest of us? That was the main argument. Most of the time I didn't argue with them. I was tired and exhausted. Everything was hard enough for me as it was. I was more concerned with the future of my child. I wanted a girl more than anything. That takes on special importance in Israel. It's not that as a woman you're more likely to identify with a girl, but rather the feeling that a girl's life is not as threatened. That's why I wanted a girl, and that's what I got.

I fear for the future of my children. We hope that everything will get better and that peace will also come to the Near East. If I had a boy I don't know what I'd do if things didn't change. I really couldn't tell you. I'd probably respect his decisions, whatever they might be, and support him.

Still and all, I don't want to live in any other country. When my husband was in prison, after the Lebanon war, I occasionally felt such despair, and we often wondered whether we oughtn't to just leave everything behind. We didn't want to be part of something we felt we couldn't accept, and we were afraid that if something were to happen here he'd have to go to jail again. In theory, that was of course a possibility, and if so, that would pose quite a problem. And so we began to act. We organized demon-

strations and wrote letters to newspapers. A peace movement sprang up in Israel. But after a year, seeing that
nothing had changed, we grew tired, and that's when we
thought of leaving.

I hope you won't misunderstand me. I'm not your stereotypical uncivil, boorish Israeli. It's hard to explain, but
I still feel like an Israeli. Many here can't accept the fact
that some of us support and love our country yet are nonetheless critical of it. They feel that anyone who criticizes
is a traitor. We are not the sort of pluralistic society you
find in other Western countries. But I was born here and
grew up here and my family has lived here for generations.
I refuse to let some narrow-minded immigrant tell me that
I and my husband aren't true patriots because we disagree
with our government. That's a stupid and ultimately de-
structive argument. I feel like an Israeli. It's the climate,
the smells, the light. Everything. I like Tel Aviv, but I could
live anywhere in Israel, not only in the city in which I was
born. I feel at home here. Everything is familiar, everything
is known.

What does the future hold in store for my children? Who
knows? At the moment things don't look so rosy. My
husband and I have withdrawn into our private world.
We're no longer involved in politics. We want to continue
our studies and organize our personal lives; we don't want
to think about politics. We're tired. Of course there are
issues beyond our personal lives. We are living in the present without giving too much thought to the future. We
have simply stopped thinking about it. The daily news
reports are repetitious, and so we hardly listen to them
anymore.

KIRSTEN

I am from Copenhagen, the child of a Danish working-class family. We were so crowded in our small apartment—there were five of us—that all I could think of was to escape from this cage. And so I didn't finish college, which put an end to my dream of becoming a dentist. I took up typing and became a secretary.

My interest in Judaism dates back to the time I worked as a baby sitter for an Orthodox Jewish family. Yiddish was the language spoken there. The father was a rabbi at the Orthodox Danish community. This, my first contact with Judaism, happened at a time of my life when I tended to romanticize many things, including Judaism.

I loved handball, and there was this Jewish sports club in Copenhagen where I used to play. There I met more Jews, and I became more and more interested in their beliefs. My family wasn't at all religious. I was baptized, and when I turned fourteen I was confirmed, but those were the only two times I'd been to church. Religion played no part in my life, although I believed in God, and when I had a problem I prayed to Him.

When I was nineteen I met an Israeli who was vacationing in Denmark, and my meeting him intensified my interest in Judaism. He spent only a few days in Denmark and then went on to the United States. Nine months later he went back to Israel, and I visited him there for a couple of weeks. I wanted to see whether I liked it, whether I thought I could live there. I loved it. Who wouldn't? I think every visitor who sees it for the first time comes away enthusiastic. I decided to go back to Denmark long enough to make some money, and then go to Israel for an extended stay. I worked in three different jobs to make money as quickly as possible, and after six months I went to Israel.

The day I got there my friend was called up to the army as a reservist and I was on my own. The first two nights I stayed at a hotel, and then I rented a room in the house of an older lady north of Tel Aviv. Then I set out looking for a job. I had begun studying Hebrew while still in Denmark. I knew the alphabet, could read a little, but spoke not a word. Being young and self-confident, and knowing some foreign languages and typing, I was lucky enough to find a job with an export-import company as an English-language secretary. Once I started working there I realized that both my English and my job skills were below par. Still, everything went well.

By the time my friend came home from the army I had become more or less integrated. I felt at home here in Israel, and after some months I decided to convert. All I wanted was to be Jewish and live in Israel, but I had no idea how many obstacles I'd have to overcome. Working and living here, learning the language, making friends, changing from the cold north to this warm country, none of that posed a problem. But becoming a Jew!

I had met a friendly, seventyish couple who became like parents. I visited them almost every day. When they heard of my plans to convert they promised to help find a rabbi to instruct me. Meanwhile I had on my own gotten in touch with the Chief Rabbi in Tel Aviv, who introduced me to an English-speaking rabbi. That was a sobering experience. He spoke to me for about fifteen minutes and then advised me to return to Denmark. He asked what I was doing in Israel and my reasons for wanting to convert. He was against it. He then asked whether I had a boyfriend, and when I told him I did he said that a conversion because of a love affair was altogether out of the question. I tried to tell him that this was something I had wanted for a long time, that it had nothing to do with my friend. But he wouldn't listen, and he most certainly didn't want to help. Later I found out that I shouldn't have let this encounter bother me so much. Everybody is turned down three times before being accepted. It's part of the game. A person truly intent on conversion won't let these repeated refusals stand in the way. But I, unfamiliar with this unwritten rule, was very upset indeed. I told my elderly friends what had happened, whereupon they introduced me to a rabbi who was ready to convert me within a week in return for two months' salary. It wasn't so much the money that bothered me as the rapidity. I thought I'd have to be introduced slowly, that I still had a lot to learn. Thanking my friends for their offer of help, I told them I'd decided to return to Denmark and seek out a rabbi there.

I stayed in Israel for another year, learned the language, and got to know the country. After that, my friend and I returned to Denmark. We both got jobs, and then I went to a Danish rabbi for help. He steered me to a teacher who taught me everything I needed to know—about observances and keeping a kosher house, all the things one has to know to lead a religious life. Now everything moved very quickly, and a few weeks later I was Jewish. I was lucky, because conversions usually take a lot longer. But having lived in Israel I was already familiar with many practices; I knew about holidays and about Judaism generally. I was twenty-three at the time. Subsequently I worked as a secretary for the Chief Rabbi in Israel.

My conversion to Judaism was more in the nature of a conversion to the Jewish way of life than to the Jewish religion. Being a believer in God though not in Jesus, I had no problem with this change. The only aspect of the Jewish religion I found disturbing was the custom of sitting shiva for the dead. I thought it very discourteous. The idea of sitting and discussing the details of the death with whoever dropped in struck me as awful. I thought that was terrible, but I've since changed my mind.

That summer I gave birth to my first son. We had married before my conversion. Later we had a religious ceremony. By marrying me, my husband was able to get a Danish work permit. The birth of my child reawakened my desire to live in Israel, the country in which I felt happy and where I wanted my child to grow up. After all, both my son and my husband were Jewish, and I wanted to live there, a place where they and I belonged. We talked about it endlessly, day and night, but we couldn't agree. Everything was topsy-turvy. My husband wanted to stay in Denmark. He loved it and was glad not to have to live in Israel anymore. And so I also stayed. We visited Israel periodically, but my desire to live there permanently didn't lessen. On the contrary.

When my second son was born it became crystal-clear to me that it was time for us to go home to Israel. My older boy was of school age, and I wanted him to go to school there. My husband promised that we would, as soon as the younger one reached school age. But when the time came he refused. He wanted to stay in Denmark; he felt at home there. I stopped arguing. It wasn't that I was unhappy in Denmark, but I couldn't help feeling that life in Israel would be better. Our children were brought up as Jews, they attended a Jewish school, we tried to give them a Jewish identity, but it all seemed like a watching a stage play, with us as the spectators. Their friends lived scattered over a wide area and visiting them was a problem. There was no community, no spontaneity. Because they didn't go to public school they had few friends in our neighborhood. My husband and I spoke Hebrew; the children understood it but they themselves spoke Danish. They were Israeli citizens but they refused to speak Hebrew.

Our marriage fell apart. I applied for Danish citizenship for my children, and it was granted a week before the three of us left for Israel. They now have dual citizenship. Our difference over whether to return to Israel or stay in Denmark was not of course the only reason we divorced. There were many more.

My husband's family had not welcomed me. I was nineteen when we met; he, twenty-four. The first time I came to Israel on vacation he took me to see his mother. She wasn't prepared for this meeting, and her rejection of me was unmistakable. The year I spent working in Israel I never met her even once. For her, I was the shiksa. I was very slender and blond. She called me that skinny, ugly girl, the one who wanted to take away her son.

My husband's parents were separated. I asked to meet his father, and he was very nice to me. We saw each other occasionally. After we went to Denmark my mother-in-law would write to my husband urging him to come back, not to stay in a country that wasn't Jewish, not to live among Gentiles. That used to annoy me, but I must admit that I now have greater understanding for her. She had come from Russia, had lived through pogroms, had gone to Poland and from there to Israel. From her perspective all Gentiles are evil beings who only want to hurt Jews. She never mentioned me in her letters, as though I didn't exist, as though my husband and I weren't living together. After I converted I wrote her a long letter without telling my husband. I wrote in Hebrew, probably a little funny, but she understood it. I told her of our marriage, of my conversion, that I was expecting a child. I tried to win her over, pleading with her not to be unhappy over my and her son's happiness, to try and accept me. I mailed the letter, and only then did I tell my husband. He almost fainted. He said that I didn't know what I was doing. But things changed after that. She wrote back that she was proud about my conversion and she was happy about the child. However, many problems still remained, such as my name, for example. "Kirsten" means Christian, and my mother-in-law just couldn't get herself to say it. She asked me what my Hebrew name was. I told her it was Tamar, and to this day that's what she and her entire family call me.

By Israeli standards I am leading a religious life here in Israel. I go to synagogue regularly and my children are being raised as religious Jews.

My own family was wonderful when I told them of my plans. And they were fond of my husband. My mother in particular was very receptive. She read everything about Judaism she could get her hands on—about Israel, about kosher households, and she got new pots to cook kosher dishes for us. Perhaps my family never really understood what was happening, but they were open and welcoming.

When did I first began to feel like an Israeli? I think from the very beginning, when I first set foot in Israel. After our divorce I told my older son that we were going to go to Israel, and some time later I also told the little one. He was violently opposed. He didn't want to leave his familiar surroundings. The older one was enthusiastic. Since I've come back to Israel my husband has begun to talk about returning, but I don't believe it. He visits us, but I'm convinced he's not going to come back for good.

I am a Dane, a convert to Judaism, living in Israel, and my sons, whom I've brought to this country after many difficulties so that they may grow up as Jews, are soldiers in an army and daily run the risk of being killed. Was it this that I was struggling for? It's a question I keep on asking myself over and over again, and there's no easy answer. The choice I made probably has as much to do with selfishness as with idealism. I knew that my sons would have to go into the army. Every day we hear about soldiers being killed by Arabs or accidentally or some other way. I don't get hysterical, but of course I worry about them more when they are serving in a dangerous zone. Yet that doesn't stop me from staying here. It's an unfortunate part of daily life. With all that, even though my sons are risking their lives for this country, I'll always be a stranger here. There are people who will never accept me. To them I'll always be the Dane.

When I came back to stay everybody spoke English with me, although my Hebrew was pretty good. Perhaps not as good as today, but still I was fluent in it. There was nothing I could do. Now only very few people still speak English with me. Why, you ask. Is it the way I act, more Israeli-like? I don't know.

I'm sure I've changed. My children say I'm Israeli, and they don't mean it as a compliment. They think the way I drive is Israeli, that I'm impatient when I have to stand in line in the supermarket. "Kirsten," the essential Kirsten, hasn't changed. My feelings are the same. I'm happy to have come here, and even when I'm beset by doubts I know that I made the right choice.

Israeli society as a whole is not very welcoming toward a woman who comes here alone with two children, but individual people are friendly. When we first came we were housed in a center for immigrants, but after a month I found both a job and an apartment. It didn't take long. I'm not angry over the difficulties I had, even though I might have preferred a smoother path. A little more information would have been welcome.

Now I am working as a teacher, and I manage somehow. There are occasional bad days, and then I think that life might be easier in Denmark, but I never seriously entertain the idea of making a change. Even though my job is well-paid I still have to do extra work one day a week to support myself and the children. It's impossible to live on my salary, at least not the way we like to.

Not many of the Israeli women I know are in my situation. Most of my friends are either married, or single, childless women. Only one of them is divorced, but her former husband contributes enough money. I think I'm the only one who's completely self-supporting.

The one thing I have trouble getting used to is the bureaucracy. If you want something from a government office it takes an eternity. You're sent from place to place. Why, you ask, aren't you ever at the right place? But you learn to be patient, even if you come from so organized a country as Denmark. And you swear and become angry—you become an Israeli.

I thought that Israel was the best place to raise children, and I still do. But I also think once they get older and have finished their army service, Israel is like any other country, except if you're an idealist. Compared to Western Europe people here aren't so well off.

My husband, a native Israeli, went to Denmark to become a millionaire. And for all I know he did. He wants to persuade his sons to return to Denmark, to study there, to become successful and make lots of money. I would like them to stay here, and for now they agree. But will I win in the end? I don't know.

AUDREY

I was the second of four children, all girls. Both my parents were born in America, as were my father's parents. Mother's came from Europe.

We were your typical American Conservative Jews, maybe a little more religious than most. Religion was as accepted a part of our life as getting up in the morning and going to bed at night. We belonged to a synagogue, celebrated all the holidays, kept a kosher house. Our Jewish identity was never in doubt. We didn't live in a Jewish neighborhood, but at home we had something like a shtetl atmosphere, largely because of Mother's Eastern European background.

Her parents and many of her older relatives were deeply involved in Yiddish culture—they spoke Yiddish, read Yiddish books, and kept going back to an almost vanished Yiddish past, to the shtetl of the Pale of Settlement. Those relatives guarded their Yiddish culture like a museum piece, an object of nostalgic reverence. However, the cause my sisters and I, even if not our parents, dedicated ourselves to was Israel and Zionism. We became active in the Zionist youth movement. To us Judaism meant Israel, the new

Jewish homeland, and because Hebrew, not Yiddish, was the language they spoke there, we went to Hebrew school, not Yiddish school. Our involvement in the Zionist youth movement became our substitute for Israel itself. Our generation, not our parents', was the one that was deeply committed to Israel.

As soon as I finished high school I went to Israel for a year as part of a group that spent five months in a kibbutz, three months in Jerusalem, and the remainder seeing the rest of the country. I gulped it down like a starving person. Everything and everybody was Jewish; everybody was like me, an incredibly heady experience for someone who hadn't grown up in a Jewish neighborhood. Suddenly I found myself in a place where the Jewish holidays were celebrated by all, where people from all sorts of backgrounds went to the synagogue. Life in a Jewish country was a source of endless wonder.

That year was over before I knew it. I returned to the United States to go to college, a halfhearted decision on my part because I didn't really know what I wanted to do. Afterward I again took off for another six months to Israel, but this time not as a sightseer. I was toying with the idea of settling there, and I wanted to look into the job situation, to find out what living there would be like. I found a job as a volunteer in a psychiatric treatment center in Jerusalem. That was a sobering experience. I got a taste of a reality for which my initial enthusiasm hadn't prepared me. The hospital I worked in was appalling, old and decrepit, and the work itself an insult to my intelligence. Their therapeutic methods were obsolete. I felt as though I was back in the infancy of medicine. Enthusiasm turned into disillusionment. But despite these catastrophic working conditions I knew I had found my profession: occupational therapy. And once I knew that's what I wanted, I returned to the States to study occupational therapy at Boston University.

In Boston, probably as a reaction to the poor working conditions in Jerusalem, my feelings about returning there began to change. Life in the Jewish state had lost some of its attraction. I was disillusioned with Zionism and everything surrounding it, and decided to devote myself to my studies. I worked hard. Israel seemed far away, even though my younger sister had moved there when she was eighteen (I was then twenty-five) and I had many friends there. After graduating I spent almost four years in New York doing occupational psychiatric counseling. I loved my work and was happy with my life.

In 1984 I went to Israel for a month, visiting my sister and seeing old friends. Suddenly all my feelings about Israel which I had pushed aside resurfaced. Buried feelings were aroused and wouldn't let go of me. It was just wonderful to be back. Within days I decided to get in touch with other therapists to find out about the psychiatric programs being used. I spoke with many professionals, including resident Americans, not so much to find out about my professional prospects but about living conditions generally. Most of the people I spoke to weren't very encouraging. As a matter of fact, they advised me against coming and opening an office here. Many were upset about the political situation, the government, the aftermath of the war in Lebanon. I heard their discouraging advice and arguments, but my mind was made up. I'm sure that there's a lot wrong here, I told myself, but it will be a new experience, and I want to become a part of it.

My decision to settle here was neither political nor religious but purely emotional. Life in Israel simply appealed to my emotions. I liked being here, found the idea of living in this young, new country exciting. Of course, now that

I'm actually living here I see things differently. But back then I felt that everyone here has the chance of playing a role in building a Jewish society, of making a contribution, that as a Jew everyone counts. I think that's what I initially found so exciting, the fact that this was a young, growing country. And a Jewish country.

It's really funny that, given my initial discouraging experience with the local working conditions, I'd find the prospect of practicing my profession in Israel exciting. And through my conversations with therapists I found out that they didn't attach the same importance to my chosen field here as in the States. Occupational therapy had begun to win recognition in the States in the early eighties. It was considered a promising approach, and funding was available. In Israel, on the other hand, funds were being cut, and because it wasn't taken seriously, it wasn't incorporated into psychiatric therapy.

I returned to America a month later, excited by the idea of moving to Israel. I planned to live near my sister and her family and my friends. I'd again be living in Israel. No sooner was I back in New York than I resumed my studies of Hebrew. Just as Israel had taken a back seat when I first embarked on my career, my profession took a back seat while I concentrated on learning Hebrew. Of course I continued to work full-time, but I no longer worried about professional advancement and other such matters. In retrospect, I must say that in the course of my life I've developed a talent for compartmentalization, at least mentally if not in practice. It seems to be something I have to do.

The year before I decided to go to Israel I'd met Charlie. He came from St. Louis from a milieu not unlike my own—a typical Conservative family a bit more religious than most. He had relatives in Israel, including a brother who had moved there in the 1970s. He himself had been to Israel a number of times, and he also planned to relocate. Charlie wanted to leave for Israel in August 1985. I had originally planned to go that spring, but professional commitments kept me in the States until the end of that year. Consequently, our plans for the big move were made separately. I needed this degree of independence, yet at the same time it was reassuring to know that our plans for the future coincided. At the time I felt it important to separate my relationship with Charlie from my move to Israel. For both of us the move and beginning a new life were an experiment with an unforeseeable outcome. There was so much that could go wrong. I didn't want to make Charlie feel responsible for my coming in case Israel didn't live up to my expectations. On the other hand, I didn't want to feel that I'd have to leave Israel in case Charlie and I broke up. This may seem a bit contrived, but my move and my relationship were two separate things.

Charlie left in August, and I in December. I missed him more than I'd thought I would; it meant a great deal to know that he'd be waiting for me when I got there. Once there, I continued to separate my profession from our relationship. And a good thing too, because soon after my arrival Charlie's mother died, and he had to return to America for an extended stay. I was temporarily on my own.

From the very beginning everything went smoothly. I made friends, and I had my work, my safety blanket. I started working as soon as I arrived, five hours a day five days a week, and adjusting to life and learning Hebrew took up whatever energy I had left.

Initially I lived in Jerusalem. I had decided on Jerusalem because I knew the city from my first visit, but I didn't really want to settle there. It's a beautiful, exciting, magical, mystical place, but I find life there too intense. In Jerusalem the country's political, social, and religious pressures are magnified tenfold. It's not a city in which I can feel at home. And my lack of talent for languages is still another reason. I realized that if I were to stay in Jerusalem I'd never learn Hebrew. In Jerusalem it's not difficult to find a job if English is your only language. It was important for me to live someplace where I'd be forced to speak Hebrew. I wanted that language to be an intrinsic part of my life in Israel.

I managed to acquire an adequate command of the professional terminology in Hebrew, just enough to help me get by in my work. Needless to say, I still feel more comfortable speaking English, and that probably won't change. I also think it important for my children to know English. Except for the people at work, English is the native tongue of most of our friends. In fact, my office is the only place I know in which Hebrew is spoken exclusively.

For a variety of reasons life here is not at all what I had thought it would be. First of all, the things that appealed to me at eighteen don't look the same at thirty-two. I discovered that trying to change a society isn't all that easy, even in so young a country as Israel. The inflexibility of bureaucracy has trickled down to all levels of operation. Naturally, approaches and practices here differ from those back in America. For example, in New York I was very active in professional associations. When I came here I found out that they either don't exist at all or they're so set in their ways that nothing has changed in the last forty years, and that new ideas and suggestions are not welcome. And in some respects the entire country is like that.

As I said earlier, Charlie and I come from Conservative families, and in the synagogues we attended women played an active role. That's something we missed here. But ever since we moved to Tel Aviv we've become active in a *chavurah*, a traditional egalitarian group that meets for study, for festivals and holidays, for parties, and for many other get-togethers. The religious structure of the *chavurah* is something in between the Orthodox synagogues and no religious affiliation whatsoever. I lost my illusions about the possibility of changing a young society long ago. Those were the dreams of a young idealist. Still, the *chavurah* has opened up the possibility of having some influence on the society, at least here in Tel Aviv.

What does it mean today, living in Israel? I was asked this question recently by a friend who lived and studied in Jerusalem near the Old City in 1987 and 1988. She had witnessed the beginning of the intifada, the elections, and many of the scandals and changes of the recent years. She was interested in knowing how things are now. The way I see it, living in Israel means just that. One learns to take in stride all the things that are happening. I have become less political because I feel that things don't change just because a thousand people demonstrate or sign petitions or rail against the government. I live from one day to the next, and that, I must confess, is easier.

Charlie's army service undoubtedly made the greatest inroads on our lives. Up to then we'd coped with a lot of minor changes, but Charlie's four months in the military raised new questions. It made both of us face up to what living here entailed. For the first time we realized that in case of a war Charlie would be called up, and that our children eventually would have to serve in the army, and not just for four months. It bothered me a lot that Adele, our two-year-old daughter, knew that her father was in the army, that he was a soldier and carried a weapon.

However, we've learned to accept all of this as a part of

life here. We were more concerned about how Charlie's four months away would disrupt our daily routine than about the big issues. And I think that holds true for everything in our life here. We give much more thought to everyday problems than to what will happen in ten or twenty years, or even in a year. As long as we don't venture beyond this level of routine existence, we're fine.

Both Charlie and I are Israeli citizens, but this business about identity is really quite strange. In the United States I felt like a Jew, not like an American. In that respect I was very different from my parents, who had grown up with the dreams about what America had to offer its immigrants. America, they felt, had been very good to them. But I didn't begin to feel like an American until I came here. Now that I'm here I feel that I'll always be an American. I grew up in New York, spent my youth there, studied and worked there. As a matter of fact, I never feel as American as when I'm in Israel. Yet when I visit America I don't feel that I belong there, and I don't think I could live there. I've grown older, my friends in New York have families, and their life differs from mine. In Israel the family is much more important. As a mother I have options that I'm sure would be foreclosed to me in New York. I'm able to work part of the time and spend time with my children. In New York I wouldn't be able to find the kind of good nursery schools and daycare centers we have here.

The children of some of our New York friends know more about Christmas than about Hanukkah, more Christmas carols than Hanukkah songs. These friends know none of the joy I experience when Adele comes home from her playgroup singing Hanukkah songs and other Hebrew melodies. These are among the reasons we're here. We may not be terribly Jewish in the eyes of the Orthodox, but that doesn't diminish my excitement over living in a Jewish society, a place where all holidays are Jewish holidays, whether you choose to observe them or not.

Yet, having said all of this, I still don't feel like an Israeli, nor do I think I ever will. I know people who've been here fifteen years and who still compare everything with "back home." They wonder and conjecture about what it would be like, and whether it mightn't be a good idea, to go back to America for a couple of years. All of us have nursed such thoughts at one time or another.

It's been four years since I came here. My sister has been here much longer. She lives in a completely Israeli milieu. Both she and her husband studied here; their children consider themselves genuine Israelis. I don't know whether she and her husband think of themselves as genuine Israelis, but in my eyes they are. I therefore was shocked when one day they began to talk of returning to America. Apparently a couple of years ago they suffered some financial setbacks. They were never particularly well off, but they always managed. But when they took stock of their situation after thirteen years here they concluded that things were becoming harder instead of easier, and they wondered whether they wouldn't be better off going back for a while to make some money.

In the end, they stayed. They decided that things wouldn't be much better for them there. They'd left the States as teenagers, and they knew that many of their ideas about America were bound to be unrealistic. I also think that they'd have great problems readjusting. Still, I can't get over my shock that they even considered returning.

But am I any different? I'm sure that however long I live here, I'll still be reading American books, most of our friends will still be Americans, we'll still like going to New York and prefer American coffee. These divided loyalties will always be part of us. My parents blame the Zionist movement for that. But I don't agree. I think it is an identity problem American Jews must come to terms with. As a Jew in America you have a pretty nebulous identity unless you belong to a group, and so you join your local synagogue. Another option is total assimilation, discarding all remnants of one's Jewish identity. I found a third option —the Zionist youth movement. Jewish identity involves more than going to a forbidding shul on Shabbat. My involvement with the Zionist youth movement and Israel was equivalent to my mother's and her generation's involvement with Yiddish culture, but the Zionist youth movement is not necessarily a steppingstone to life in Israel. Some of its most passionate adherents leave Israel again, while others who come here for a variety of nonideological reasons decide to stay and become citizens. Perhaps because they don't come with the same expectations as the Zionists they also don't become as disillusioned.

I think I fit in somewhere between these two extremes. True, I had expectations, but because I'd talked to people who were living here, I wasn't so wide-eyed when I came. And it would be unfair to hold Israel responsible for some of my early disappointments. Living in a new country, learning a new language, making new friends, finding a professional foothold, all those, except for the language, are problems I might have faced had I moved to California instead.

Charlie's ties and mine to America are still close, but we want our children to grow up in Israel even though we know that life here doesn't offer them the same possibilities as America. Of course, they're still very young, and we're not sure how we'll feel when they're eighteen and have to go into the army. There are times when I ask myself whether we've done right by them. On the other hand, I feel that for the time being they have a good life. Not only are the nursery schools better here, but they are growing up with an unambiguous Jewish, Israeli identity. Of course we make decisions on behalf of our children, but that would be true wherever we lived. I am convinced that it is better for them to grow up here than in New York, but the final decision of where to live once they are older is up to them.

Our children are aware that their parents are different, that they're Americans, and that therefore they too are different. We speak English, we have English-speaking friends, and we want them to learn English. Sometimes I feel a little guilty. When Adele was in nursery school she was just beginning to talk, and I asked myself, What are we doing to this poor child? Learning one language is hard enough, and now we want her to learn two. But now that I see that it's no problem for her I tell myself that we didn't do anything terrible. On the whole I feel that our decision to live and raise our children here was the right one. Of course, I can't say how I'll feel about it later, not only because of the army but also because they are certain to find out how difficult, problem-ridden, and short life here can be. I don't know how I'll feel about all of this ten years from now.

RUTH

I am a sixth-year medical student. When I was about seventeen or eighteen an uncle of mine suddenly turned religious and moved his entire family to Jerusalem. My parents went the opposite way; they turned away from religion, even though they risked tearing the family apart. As for me, the subject of religion came to occupy me more and more. I experimented with various approaches. A Jew, I'd say to myself, can be religious without observing the laws and still be a good person. However, I didn't find this argument altogether convincing. Shortly before being called up to the army I heard a lecture by a rabbi, I no longer remember who. But after listening to him I went outside, looked up into the sky, and then looked down again. I saw the crowd of people, and caught in the middle there was I, a girl, a young woman, and I thought to myself, If in your innermost being you want to be at peace with yourself and find the way that is right for you, then this is it. Okay. And right there and then I reached the decision to become not merely pious but Orthodox, not merely to believe but to observe all the Jewish laws. Now I live in a religious kibbutz, Kibbutz Saad.

I was born in a kibbutz on Lake Genezareth. My parents, who had come here in 1958 from Argentina, spent their first twelve years there. I was seven when they left and moved to the city. I have wonderful memories of my childhood in the kibbutz. Never again did I feel so close to nature. I spent more time outdoors than in, becoming a part of nature, changing along with the changing seasons.

That kibbutz was not religious, but it would be wrong to say that my parents weren't religious. Things can't be compartmentalized so rigidly; it's not a matter of either/or. Nor did my turn to religion happen overnight. It's not as though I woke up one morning, opened my eyes, and suddenly saw the light. There's bound to be something wrong with any such rapid change. Going over from one belief, from one way of life, to another is a gradual process.

My parents didn't observe the laws, yet I'm sure they were religious. There is belief, and then there is observance of the laws. Many people settle for belief alone, think of themselves as believers even though they do not keep a kosher house and don't observe the Sabbath. They close an eye. My parents decided on which laws to follow and which to ignore, and their list of observances continued to shrink. I wouldn't say that my sister was impious, but rather that she was unbelieving. When we were youngsters we moved in different circles, and later we went our separate ways.

I'd always felt a need to be observant, but I didn't really commit myself until hearing that rabbi. I told myself that if I am to have a sense of wholeness, if I am to become an integrated, thoughtful human being, then the way I think and the way I act must also be brought into harmony.

Then came my military service and I had to postpone all decisions about my future. I hadn't confided my ideas about religion to anybody, not even my parents. I wanted to arrive at an answer to these questions by myself, without any outside influence. My two years in the army were a very busy time for me, leaving little room for contemplation. Toward the end of my stint I met Ron; we had served in the same unit for six months.

I was apprehensive about life after the army. I'd heard from others about the difficulties they'd had adjusting after leaving that closed community, of facing real life, of being responsible for themselves. And I was also apprehensive because of my religious feelings. I feared that my turn to religion would change my life completely. I felt like a spaceship torn out of its orbit, left to navigate on its own. Suddenly I would no longer be able to go to my favorite haunts and would have to spend my evenings alone. My old friends would become distant, relationships would break off, my old world would become more and more strange. And what I feared more than anything was becoming estranged from my family. I figured that they wouldn't welcome my decision, and I was afraid of their criticism, for I knew how easily influenced I was. In the army I'd met some girls from religious families, and they actually were the strongest ones. They had such tremendous inner strength; I admired them.

Ron had none of my problems. Having grown up in an observant household, he had lived with religion since childhood, and so he took it all for granted. Something I was laboring to master was as natural to him as getting up in the morning. For me it was like putting on a pair of magic glasses and suddenly seeing my surroundings turn into something I'd dreamed about as a child. I loved being with Ron. He was the personification of my fantasy. All I had to do was watch him and follow his lead. He made things very simple for me. I knew that I could live with him the way I had always dreamed of. The two of us moved into the religious kibbutz. Everything changed for me—my friends, the food I ate, life itself. My Zionist-Jewish environment became my new home.

My turn toward religion also changed my attitude toward my nation and toward Israel. I look at this state and ask myself, Who are these people who for millenniums have managed to preserve their culture? It must be their religion. The rules of their belief are the cement that holds everything together. Not the idea or the theory of their religion or their feeling of community, but the laws, the rituals, the strict rules. We Jews are an incredibly rigid people. Religious commands often also make for a rigid family structure, barring its individual members from simply going their own way. There's the Sabbath, at which everyone must be present. And the sexual rules are a stimulus rather than a obstacle. Judaism also has no room for trendiness. Our customs are ancient and unchanging.

I know we are living in a very free age. People don't want to be dictated to. Rules and laws are considered old-fashioned, burdens from the past. But as far as I'm concerned these rules are the framework holding our very life together and making it beautiful. It's not enough to be the owner of an Israeli passport or to know that you're Jewish. Naturally, above all, I'm Jewish, or else I wouldn't be an Israeli. If I weren't living here everything would be meaningless. Being a Jew is not a matter of attitude or political opinion. It's something that cannot be discarded or altered or traded away. It is an affiliation I cannot throw off.

My parents sacrificed a great deal to come to this country. I honor and respect them for it, but I now feel that I bear a responsibility for the future. It is time for me to take history into my own hands. I turned to religion not because

I felt desperate or in need of a crutch. My life was going very well.

Ron grew up here, in this kibbutz. Children here lead an ideal religious existence, and the old people are looked after. However, for us, the in-between generation, things are a bit more problematic. We're a minority. Actually, I wanted to leave the kibbutz and move to the very religious section of the city, but Ron grew up here, and he felt he owed it to the community to stay and help in case he was needed, and so we stayed. He feels responsible for everything happening here. It's like one great big family.

I have two children, aged four and five, and for them it's wonderful here, far better than in the city. Still, I feel ambivalent about the kibbutz. Maybe one day we'll go away. Religious or not, a kibbutz is still a kibbutz, and the organization is not structured for everyone. The communal religion is lovely. We have our own synagogue and attend prayers three times a day. Sabbath services are held in the big dining hall; a communal kiddush is said, and everybody joins in the prayer at the end of the meal. Those are the attractive aspects of life here. However, not every family here is religious, only the kibbutz itself. I think I'd prefer life in a still more religious setting. There is a certain lack of profundity. Many things here are automatic; very few of the members give much thought to the reason of existence. In the community, religion tends to become a matter of outward appearance. It does not enter into decision-making, though you might think that it ought to be important. Perhaps both my demands and my expectations are too high. I constantly feel the difference between someone like myself who came to religion later in life and someone who grew up with it. I don't have that matter-of-fact attitude. I am much more strict and forever worrying about making a mistake. Maybe I'm not relaxed enough.

I was studying medicine when I married into the kibbutz. Nobody can interfere with my studies now, though I'm sure they would have had I moved here earlier. But under the circumstances I didn't need permission. This is one of the areas where religion is also misunderstood. We may be religious, but we live like anybody else. We want to read the same books as others and watch the things they watch. We want to keep our minds open to things not written in the Torah. So many preconceptions about us have gained currency, even though religious people are to be found everywhere, at the movies and basketball games, at bookstores and at political rallies. Yet that doesn't stop the spread of those stereotypical ideas that all they do is study Torah day and night.

I had my problems at the university. I wear a head covering, and at first everybody was surprised to find an Orthodox woman studying medicine. The first year was very difficult. I felt as though I was moving between two different worlds. It's easy to feel isolated, left out, when a fellow student on a Monday morning tells about her wild weekend. It's as though we're speaking a different language. And I can't share my life with the others.

However, these are superficial problems and not all that important. What matters is my inner life, and that's where I am still up against a wall. I keep on yearning for a religious world of ideas, for becoming steeped in it. When I first began my quest for religion Ron and I enrolled in some courses in Jerusalem. They didn't deal with observance. I didn't go there to learn how to keep a kosher house. We were looking for inner stability; the observances were simply ornaments. What remains basic is the fascinating diversity of the Jewish faith. Everyone is given the option of going his or her own way. Unlike the majority of Orthodox Jews I joined the army and went into a profession. I don't think there exists a Jew with no belief at all. In some way every Jew is religious. And those who say they do not believe probably give the idea of religion more thought than the believers. And that means they are on the right road.

ROBERT

It was the Friday evening after my high school finals, which I managed to pass by the skin of my teeth. Uncle Amnon was visiting, as he did every Friday when he was in the city. Everything was as usual. After the kiddush, Mother served the traditional fish and soup. Uncle Amnon congratulated me and asked what I planned to do now that I had graduated. I looked at Father, he looked at me; I looked at Mother, she looked at Father. I said I was planning to go to Israel. The rest of the meal was eaten in silence. When we finished Mother pushed back her chair and said, "He wants to go to the only country in the world where Jews are still being killed." It was the summer of 1967, shortly after the Six-Day War. In September I left for Israel.

Both my parents came from Poland, from Warsaw. They had met after the war in a Red Cross camp. My father is an incredibly powerful man. At eighty his hands are still strong, his back is ramrod-straight. Having fought and survived the Warsaw ghetto, he doesn't accept defeat. He says that even death does not mean defeat if you defend yourself, and if the last thing you do is to spit in the face of your enemy you have defeated him even though he may kill you. That is the meaning of heroism, the lesson he taught me.

After the war my parents stayed in Berlin. Father went into the moving business; it failed. Later he took a job in a friend's business. Mother is a gentle creature. A survivor of the camps, she concentrated all her emotions on her children. She was always there for us.

Religion never was an issue in our house. Father had been a dedicated Communist, but that's a thing of the past. Not only had his politics colored his attitude toward religion but toward Israel as well. I was raised as an anti-Zionist. In my early youth I was violently pro-Arab, not like today's leftists in Israel who call for dialogue and negotiations. Much worse. In my innermost heart I sympathized with PLO terrorism. I saw it as akin to choosing between the Americans and the Russians. Be that as it may, one thing was certain—I didn't support the Israelis.

Mother in a way was religious. If she didn't observe anything it was out of deference to Father. When I was little we observed nothing, no holidays, no Friday evenings, no Sabbaths, nothing, and of course, not Christmas either. Communists believed in nothing, not even Santa Claus. But then came the Hungarian revolution, and Father's view began to undergo a change, and when Stalin's crimes became public knowledge he left the Communist Party. Being still very young, I didn't understand any of this.

One day Father took me for a walk, pointed to a building, and said, "That's a synagogue." Okay, so it's a synagogue. It meant no more to me than any other public building. He tried to explain that it was something like a church, a church for Jews. And, sort of offhand, he informed me that we were Jews, which also meant nothing to me.

But as time went on, Mother began to assert herself more and more, and Father didn't interfere. He let her have her way. And when she suggested that perhaps we ought to light candles on Friday, he didn't object. The very next day he came home lugging a bulky tote bag out of which he took two candlesticks, a kiddush cup, a cloth for bread, and a book. I looked at the book but couldn't make it out. He took it from me and began to read from it. It was the first time I saw my mother cry.

That is how religion first entered into our home. After that on Fridays we would gather at home together with some relatives and friends. My biggest surprise was to find out that Father could read Hebrew. Of course, when he was young knowing Hebrew was a given.

When I was fourteen Uncle Amnon took me on my first visit to Israel. He came from Hungary. He's a little older than Father, and when I was a boy he became a sort of substitute grandfather. My grandparents had been killed. Like my father, Uncle Amnon was a Communist, and he'd led an adventurous life, including fighting in the Spanish Civil War. From Spain he went to the Soviet Union, where he worked in a prison camp, trying to convert the German Nazi war prisoners to communism. After the war he came to Berlin. He left the party together with my father. He was the only Jew I knew who always had a German shepherd in tow. Mother hated that animal and would not let it into the apartment.

Well, Uncle Amnon took me to Israel, and here all my mixed-up feelings about being a member of a minority disappeared. Suddenly I was one among many like me. My family's substitution of Judaism for communism solidified my minority status. Before, I used to defend the Russians, right or wrong. I was to find out that the special position of being Jewish had a similar effect. The other kids at school, and especially the girls, were fascinated. Nothing is more interesting than being different from other boys of the same age. But in Israel everybody is different and yet alike. You can't be more different than the people here. Every degree of difference you can think of is to be found here. Communist? Jew? They'd just laugh. What's so special about that?

It was wonderful, all that laughter, especially for someone from Berlin, that glum, gray city full of glum, gray people. Here, in this southern country, everything was so open. When I came back to Berlin and told my parents that I wanted to go to Israel they just smiled indulgently. They didn't take me seriously. But when I began to study Hebrew they became uneasy. They would have accepted any other country, even America, despite their leftist past. But Israel frightened them. I don't know exactly whether it was the threat of war or that buried fear that I'd turn into a real Jew. But I was determined.

Then I began to date a girl in Berlin. She wasn't Jewish, and my parents were delighted. I think they hoped that this would put an end to my notions about Israel. Gitta—that's her name—was extremely interested in Judaism. When she came to our house she would ask hundreds of questions. She wanted to know everything. A year before my graduation the two of us went to Israel for our summer vacation. It was tough. We worked in an orange plantation in a kibbutz. Gitta was enthusiastic about everything, and I, who loved it there and wanted to stay, began to tear everything down just for the sake of argument. I couldn't stand her romanticization, the flip side of anti-Semitism. In Berlin I didn't mind it too much. It was nice to be admired for being different. But here? Here everybody's like this. You can't admire a sleazy operator just because he's a Jew, and here there were plenty of sleazy operators.

When I returned home at the end of August I knew that my choice was clear: either stay in Germany with Gitta or go to Israel without her. After my graduation I left, without Gitta. I wanted to study in Israel, and my parents supported me. Life was wonderful and difficult. I found an inexpensive room in the home of a Moroccan woman, left the kibbutz, and began my studies. First of all, before I could register for my courses—my field was German studies—I had to learn Hebrew.

My landlady was very unlike any of the other Jewish women I'd met. She was widowed. Her husband had been killed in the Six-Day War. He had escaped from an Arab country only to be killed fighting Arabs. She was short and dark. She looked like an Arab. And boy, could she curse! Her voice would grow hoarse, and you'd think she was on the verge of collapse. But she didn't collapse, and when the storm blew over she was her old happy, friendly self again.

Once when I came home I found her lying on the tiles in the kitchen. I rushed over and grabbed her by the shoulder. She turned around, and pushing my hand away, she screamed at me to leave her alone. Was I in the habit of attacking helpless women? she asked. And having gotten that off her chest, she informed me that when it was hot she always lay down on the floor, the one cool spot in the house. She was a crazy, good-natured woman.

Eventually I joined the army and wore my uniform proudly. After all the years in that lousy Germany my life underwent a radical change. I was rid of all this Berlin psychobabble about one's mental health, about problems and depressions, about unresolved relationships to one's parents, to authority, to history, to the past.

The Holocaust–postwar ego trip had finally come to an end for me. The uniform I was wearing was reality. I was a soldier; I now had a homeland, far away from Germany, far away from the neurotic survivors and their children who had returned to the country of their murderers. That's how I felt, at least then.

But by the time of the Yom Kippur War I realized that I hadn't really escaped the post-Holocaust syndrome. The talk in Israel was not about a war, about enemy soldiers who had to be defeated, but about the threat of annihilation. The Final Solution was omnipresent. The fear was not fear of military defeat but of extermination.

The war lasted two weeks, and unlike my father, that survivor among the defeated, I was on the side of the victors. I was a hero who was celebrated for what he had done, not merely for having survived. I will never forget Golda Meir's speech, in which she said we must win because we must live, that our enemies aren't fighting for their lives and their independence but to exterminate us. That war turned me into an Israeli, and the Arabs into my enemies. I had made a 180-degree turn.

My best friend in the army was a boy by the name of Erwin, a ridiculous German name. He also was born in Germany, and had emigrated to Israel while still a teenager. He was a radio operator in my unit. He was captured by the Syrians. We found him some days later. They'd put a pistol to his head and killed him after taking him prisoner.

I stayed in Israel and got married. My wife is from Austria. Her parents still live in Vienna. She came here almost fifteen years ago to study. We found that our cultural background was different from that of many of the people here. That was something very nice, and still is. We can talk about Kafka and get mad about things we read in the *Spiegel*, and still be Israelis. I teach at the university and my wife works in a pharmacy. We have two children, a boy and a girl. When we got married we moved to Tel

Aviv. We were lucky to be able to get a small house. It's not all that easy, but both our parents helped us. We'd never have managed it on our own.

I was called up for reserve duty a number of times, in the course of which I also served in Lebanon. Three years ago my small detachment was stationed on top of a hill in south Lebanon. We had one cannon that was able to spot and aim at moving objects even in the dark (I hope I'm not revealing any military secrets). In the morning we could see whether we'd made fools of ourselves or whether there was a funeral. But nothing shook me; I'd become hard. Arabs were and are my enemy.

The next year I served in the occupied territories. That was an entirely new, and dreadful, experience. The people I was facing weren't enemy soldiers but women and children. They sent the children over to us, little boys throwing stones. Or they'd come over toward us, smiling, innocent, empty-handed, speaking fluent Hebrew. Your mother is a whore, they'd say, and so's your sister. We'll fuck your mother in the ass a ten-year-old kept on saying over and over again. Where did he learn this? Who sent him into war instead of shielding him from war? What kind of mothers are these that send their children into such danger? Up to now only the Nazis did this sort of thing, and then only in the final hours before their surrender.

One day we came to a village we suspected of harboring terrorists. We searched the houses. Always the same scene: screaming, crying women. But my pity dried up a long time ago. Who can still believe a crying woman who sends her children out against armed soldiers? We combed the houses and drove the men out on the road, lined them up with their backs against the wall, and searched them. And while we were doing this the children threw stones at us. A soldier standing next to me collapsed, his face covered with blood.

I gave the order to fire over the heads of the children, and they disappeared as quickly as they had come. And then suddenly I heard a loud noise, and flames and smoke everywhere. I felt a sharp pain in my hand. The next thing I knew I was lying on a hospital bed and a doctor was bending over me, smiling. I nodded at him and smiled back. And then some more doctors and nurses came in, all of them smiling and making soothing noises. I knew right away that something was seriously wrong, and when I tried to sit up I realized that my left arm wasn't there.

When I was discharged from the hospital I immediately returned to work. I was determined to lead a normal life. I wouldn't let my wife and children baby me; everything was to go on as normally as possible. That proved to be a blessing. I also continued to help with household chores, wash dishes, set the table, repair dripping faucets.

I continued to live normally. I stayed on in Israel. It's my country. I haven't told my parents of my injury. They are quite old, and I see them only once or twice a year. Until now I've managed to fool them with my artificial arm. It's a macabre game. I try to keep Mother from touching my left arm. Thank God it's not the right side. I would never have believed how unimportant the left arm can become if the right one is trained to take over.

Still, there's no denying that I'm a cripple. My left stump dangles from my shoulder like a fat little sausage. I never found out exactly what actually happened, but apparently a Molotov cocktail had exploded right next to me. I've often asked myself whether all this was necessary. My parents had barely survived, and now here I was sacrificing myself. There's no answer except to keep going.

I now support Israel's hard-liners more than ever. You can't trust a people that sends its children to wage war. The intifada is a war directed against us Jews, and we must fight the uprising like any other war. We can't negotiate just because the world wants us to. Maybe later, but not now. Where was that world when my grandparents were being slaughtered? Where was it in 1967? And where will it be when Syrian tanks roll against us from a new Palestinian state? Promises will not protect us. We will always be alone; that's why we can make agreements only with people who respect us, not with people whose sole aim is to exterminate us.

A Palestinian state? What's that supposed to mean? If there is to be such a state it's in Jordan, not here. And if I had to fight again with only one arm I'd do it. I won't let the Arabs kill me. What my parents and the rest of my family went through is enough to last for the next thousand years. This had been the land of the Jews for more than a thousand years until they were driven out, into the Diaspora, into the Holocaust. Never again! The Israeli who is saying this to you may have only one arm, but don't underestimate his determination.

ANDRÉ

My kibbutz is on a hillside in northern Israel, not far from Haifa and Mount Carmel. There's a place there from which, weather permitting, I can look all the way to Tel Aviv in the south, and to the hills of Galilee and Mount Hermon, covered with snow in winter, to the north. Standing amidst scented, blossoming orange groves I can see green hillsides and snow-covered mountains. This must be the most beautiful place on earth.

I've lived in this kibbutz all my life. My father came here from Bulgaria in 1936. My mother of blessed memory was born in Latvia, and like my father belonged to the Shomer Hazair.

I am the oldest of four brothers. All of us married women from the outside and brought them to the kibbutz, and all of us still live here. Thirteen grandchildren keep my father very busy. I have four sons; the oldest, who is twenty, is an officer in a tank unit.

I grew up and attended school in this kibbutz. This is the only life I know, and chances are this is where I'll stay.

Our small, closed world is not untouched by what is happening on the outside, yet ours is an almost unreal, idyllic existence. I was born during the Second World War, but our settlement was not touched by the war. Whatever was happening then was far away. Even my parents only knew about what was going on outside by reading about it in books and newspapers. The Holocaust did not have the same immediacy for us as the later wars here in Israel.

Even though I was still very young at the time of the War of Independence, I remember how the Egyptian planes attacked a British post not far from here. Our air force pursued the Egyptians and downed one of their aircraft. I remember riding through the fields on a jeep with my father and some other men to look at the burning wreck, a reeking heap of metal sitting in a scorched field.

I was the first child born in this kibbutz. Would you really have called it a kibbutz back then? Actually, it was nothing but a treeless, arid, rocky hillside, not the paradise of green meadows, fields, and tall trees you see now. Visitors who come and gape say that we chose the most beautiful place in all of Israel. They don't know what it looked like in the beginning.

In the early days there were only few children here. We grew up together with the newly planted trees. In the darkness—the streets were unlit—these small trees looked like savage beasts to me. In winter the roads were muddy, and in the summer thistles grew everywhere. We children lived in the so-called children's house. At night I'd get frightened and run over to my parents, and when I got there I'd be covered with scratches. The early sanitary facilities weren't great; many families shared single rooms, and men and women took turns using the few showers there were. The kibbutz, the same age as I, was being built by people fired by enthusiasm and euphoria.

Our hillside was surrounded by a cluster of Arab villages. The early settlers bought land from the Arabs and built their kibbutzim. My parents had bought their land from the Arabs seven years before our kibbutz was founded. A small wooded strip encircling the hill was the boundary between us and the Arab villages. Coexistence was the norm. Both ownership and boundaries were clearly defined, and there was nothing equivocal about the land purchases.

During the War of Independence we implored the Arabs to stay. After all, we'd been neighbors and had never had any problems. But the Arab leaders agitated against us and made false promises to their charges. They told them that if they'd leave their villages temporarily they'd not only get their own land back but also captured territory. But we Jews had paid for every grain of sand. When I was little I was not afraid of the Arabs. I don't think any of us were. I saw them every day; we were next-door neighbors.

Even though in the beginning our kibbutz had nothing, we children wanted for nothing. The first houses built were the children's houses. Ours was heated. The mothers only came to nurse their babies or for visits. However, over the years the practice of separating children and parents changed, and with it a number of related habits. Thus, we two older brothers, who were brought up in a children's house, still called our parents by their first names, but the two younger ones called them Papa and Momma. As time went on the trend was toward the nuclear family, which caused a problem not only ideologically but also financially. It is less expensive to have a group of children sleep in one place than in separate children's rooms in every household. Even today, children over the age of two cannot sleep in their parents' house. However, things aren't all that strict anymore. When one of my sons was afraid of sleeping in the children's house we took him home with us. After a while he asked to return to the children.

When the children reach high school age they are sent to kibbutz boarding schools with about three hundred to four hundred students. They love it. All that independence and the chance to escape close parental control. Besides their schoolwork they also have to work in agriculture. The younger ones visit with their parents every day; the older ones have no rules. The eighteen-year-old Israelis who leave the kibbutz at the end of their schooling are adults, not children. They have studied and worked and learned how to be on their own, and when they join the army they have no problems.

I was one of fifty boys here who went directly from school into the army. It was the first time that I met young Israelis from the outside. That's when I first realized how isolated my life in the kibbutz had been. It was also my first encounter with Oriental Jews, with immigrants from faraway lands, representatives of all the various groups of Israeli society. In the army I felt for the first time that Israel was a nation.

I did well in the military. I took course after course, became a commissioned officer in a parachute unit, and then was put in command of an officers' training group. Nowadays it is usual for a young person to be part of a youth group in the city before joining the army, to learn how to work with others. My second son did just that for a year before going into the army. Israelis used to think of the typical kibbutznik as somebody with a *kova tembel*, that funny little cap, on his head and clutching an orange in his hand. That romanticized image was never accurate. Nowadays the kibbutz is an open society. We here can be in Haifa or Tel Aviv in no time at all, and we have our own apartments with TVs and VCRs and stereos.

When I was young and we wanted to listen to rock-and-roll we had to do it secretly. To admit to liking that kind of music was tantamount to a betrayal of the socialism we were going to build here. Today it seems ridiculous. Pop singers now give concerts here. There's been so much change. The majority of the people here were Ashkenazim and intermarried, and obviously the offspring of these unions weren't Yemenis. But there came a time when the kibbutz began to take in abandoned and orphaned children, and they grew up with our own children and became part of the kibbutz. Many stayed, married, and had children. At first there were problems, primarily with the older Ashkenazim, many of whom wouldn't allow their children to marry these newcomers, and there were some Romeo and Juliet tragedies, young men in love with dark-skinned girls meeting in secret, and mothers following their sons to see what they were up to—not exactly the realization of socialism. But that's no longer so. We now have kibbutzniks from Yemen and Morocco and Tunisia. Our society has changed radically.

I personally have no problem with the Arabs. I've known them from childhood on; they've been here all along, just like us. Yet things have changed. The tension is tangible, and there are problems, and always there is a feeling of apprehension. However, I try as best I can to work for peace. I don't want a war with the Arabs. All I want is peace. I talk with my Arab friends—I have quite a few— yet at the same time all my sons are in the army. It's not simple. I want peace, but more than anything I don't want any of my sons to be killed. But they will have to fight, regardless of the cost in lives.

This is a never-ending topic here. We talk to our Arab neighbors and I say to them we have a problem as Jews and you have a problem as Arabs. We talk about possible solutions and we understand each other, but then I get called up to the reserves. As a high-ranking officer I don't just sit at a desk. I command and give orders to soldiers and am responsible for a specific campaign or even for an entire sector. I make decisions that stand in complete contradiction to my dreams of peace. I hand down orders to young soldiers fighting Arabs. And when I get back home and take off my uniform, I sit down and drink tea with Arabs, and we philosophize about peace. It's not easy. I will continue to be called up until I'm fifty, and after that my sons will still be here and serve in the army. Nobody here is ever just a civilian. Every theory about war or peace turns to bitter reality if you yourself or your children wear a uniform. And after that come your grandchildren. When will it all end?

There was a time when Jews said that Israel was the safest place in the world for them. Now many immigrants, particularly those from Russia, try to get a visa for Canada or the United States. The endless hostilities also have made it difficult for the young generation to believe as wholeheartedly in the country as we did. The fact that many young people want to leave is the greatest tragedy of our country. We should stop laying down so many conditions when peace is at stake. We can't last this way much longer. This year alone almost twenty thousand young people are expected to leave. That hurts someone like me who has helped build the kibbutz, fought in the army, and believes in his country. Now for the first time I fear for my land.

I was born here and have spent my life here. I am luckier than most other Jews in this century: I have a homeland, a country in which I live, that I have worked for. When I walk out of my house I see this lovely landscape, a scene that changes with the seasons. I have sentimental ties to this land. I'm not religious. We celebrate only the major holidays. But I have a deep belief that this is our land and has been for generations. We have not been forced to come here, to live in a ghetto in an alien land, as was the case in other parts of the world. We belong here. And that also holds true of the territories, despite all the problems there. We have the right to live there; we must not give them up. I know, there has to be a compromise, but not one that means that Jews once more must have to leave. Not again! We must bring up our children so that they again can live next to their Arab neighbors. We've spent years turning our young into the best fighters in the world. It is now time for them to develop other skills. A future government must integrate the Arabs. But who is there to make this decision? Since the founding of the state we have raised three generations of soldiers. Negotiation and compromise were not part of their curriculum.

Soon all my sons will be in the army, but they also demonstrate with the Peace Now group. That's because we took them along with us to demonstrations while they were still babes in arms. We tried to raise them as proud Israelis who loved their country but who could think for themselves and stand up for their beliefs. Still, I cannot help worrying. This past year twenty young men from this kibbutz have left the country.

ORNA

There's nothing special about my life. It can be summed up in one short sentence. I'm your typical, average Israeli who has neither suffered any great trauma nor nurses any unfulfilled yearnings. All I want is to lead a normal, well-ordered life. Having said that, I've covered the entire range of normality, because it's impossible to live a financially secure life in Israel without engaging in some shady business. And if you're a doctor that's the last thing you want to do.

Both my parents came to Israel from Rumania in their youth at the end of the Second World War. They met at a kibbutz and got married. I have an older sister who was born in 1947.

In the war my mother worked in the Underground in Rumania, ferrying the children of deportees to Palestine. Even though Jews in Rumania were comparatively safe and not being exterminated en masse, Mother witnessed many tragic cases. By some twist of fate, it was she who got my father the documents he needed for his emigration.

I was born in 1954. I was probably an accident, because Mother didn't want any more children. Having worked in the Underground, she may not be your typical Holocaust victim, but that doesn't mean that she didn't have deep-seated fears. Like almost everybody else here, she had lost relatives in the Holocaust. And no sooner had she come here to freedom and married than, a year after my sister was born, my father went off to fight in the War of Independence. After being wounded he was exempted from future military service.

When I was seven my parents left the kibbutz, mostly for political and personal reasons. A number of their closest friends had already left and they felt isolated. The kibbutz was riddled with ideological conflicts: Socialists versus Communists; profamily against antifamily. We moved to a suburb of Haifa, a rather drab, industrialized section with many ex-kibbutzniks. My father was a construction engineer, which meant that we had a steady income. My mother had worked in a kindergarten in the kibbutz, but lacking professional credentials, she had to take additional courses in order to keep working in her field.

Back then, people who left the kibbutz community were not treated as tenderly as nowadays, when people who leave get severance payments based on the length of time they've worked in their kibbutz. By contrast, when my parents left they had to compensate the kibbutz for their training. That wasn't all that easy for a couple with two young children trying to establish themselves. My parents worked hard, but they felt it was worth it. On the whole, mine was a happy childhood. The move from the kibbutz to the city didn't bother me, and I don't remember ever hearing my parents discuss their financial worries in front of us.

Only later—I was then about fifteen—did I find out about their problems, about the money they owed the kibbutz and the difficulties they had making a fresh start. I suppose that experience explains their determination to make their children self-sufficient.

Other than that, there's nothing much to tell about my childhood and youth. Like all the other children in our neighborhood I joined a Socialist youth group when I was ten. Haifa was known as the Red City. However, that doesn't mean we were involved in big political activities. Our group was just a place for children to meet and spend their free time. Nobody ever talked about politics. We might have had some political discussions later on, as high school seniors, but even those were rather tame since all of us came from Socialist families and there wasn't a great deal of dissension.

I began my military service a year before the Yom Kippur War, but not as part of the regular army. Instead, I became a group leader of twelfth-year students who, six months before being called up, spend a week playing soldier as a preparation for army life. It's more like a youth camp than the army. You go on hikes, sleep in tents, sit around campfires and sing. Ever since then I've had my fill of nature and the outdoors. Somewhere in my mind I connect hiking and camping with the military and I don't particularly enjoy it.

After my military service I went to Tel Aviv and enrolled in medical school. Because I didn't want to take any money from my parents I went to work in the hospital as a nurse's aide. However, in Israel it's possible to be on your own only if you're either very rich or very poor. When I applied for student housing they asked for proof of my parents' income, and that was too high for me to get into the dorm. I tried to tell them that my parents weren't all that well off and couldn't support me even if I wanted them to. And so I took on more work and shared living quarters with two other students. In the hospital I met my husband. He's also a medical doctor, the father of two children from a previous marriage.

After finishing medical school I gave birth to my first child even before I began my hospital stint with the attendant night duty and irregular hours. Our second daughter was born four years ago. What with night duty and other problems, the family life of two physicians is hard enough. Moreover, doctors here make very little money. We can't afford to buy an apartment, we have no saving accounts on which to fall back in an emergency. We've had to sell our car; we just couldn't afford it any longer. Vacations abroad are out of the question.

My parents and the parents of my husband have enough to live decently, but they can't help us out. Rents here are astronomical, which means that almost all our money goes toward rent and childcare. In a few months I'll get my certification in internal medicine, but it's practically impossible to get admitted to private practice. Everything goes via the health service and unions. I'll probably have to look for another job, perhaps with an insurance or pharmaceutical company. All my life I've wanted to do something that satisfies me. But what good is satisfaction in a profession that can't support you economically?

My husband also decided to leave the hospital. He's now an orthopedist in the army. The pay in the military and the many perks professional soldiers enjoy are far better. There was a time when doctors here fought for their rights. Many still talk of the big doctors' strike. But now there's nothing but frustration and everybody looks for a second or off-the-book job to help make ends meet.

Still, I'm not thinking of leaving or of going to America, like so many of my colleagues. This is my home. I'm attached to this country despite all the difficulties. Israel is like a game of chance for grown-ups. Making it here is challenging.

Of course I'm a Zionist, even if a disappointed one. Not only is the economic condition of academics frustrating; the political condition of our country doesn't exactly fill me with enthusiasm. On the contrary. I'm ashamed of my government, of my army, and of my people who keep on electing this government.

I now am to the left of the Socialist Party. In my student days I was an extreme leftist. My friends and I were engaged in a sort of masochistic self-laceration, questioning the very right of Jews to be on this land. We saw ourselves as the only group of people determined to stir up a smug population. Obviously, back then I wasn't a Zionist.

Now I no longer see things this black-and-white. It is, I believe, self-evident that Jews have a right to be here, not because of a Biblical past but because my parents' generation and others before them built this land. Where should we go? Back to Rumania, where my parents came from? Where is an Israeli whose parents came from Poland or from Iraq supposed to go?

There is no way back. We are a mixture of peoples and cultures out of which evolved a new unity and a new identity. Many on the outside don't understand this. I'm convinced that an Israeli nation has come into being, and that cannot be undone. No amount of criticism and unease can change the fact that many of my generation would do everything in their power to safeguard and defend this people and this country. We are probably not as uncritical as the founder generation, as our parents, but the basic attitude hasn't changed all that much, even if many young people want to leave.

On the other hand, as far as the territories are concerned,

I personally don't need them, neither with nor without Jewish settlers. For all I care, let them stay there once the Israeli army pulls out. If that soil is so sacred to them, they can also live there with a Jordanian passport or a Palestinian passport. They won't be worse off than Arabs with Israeli passports. The mere fact that we've been sitting there for twenty years doesn't mean that we have a legal right.

The damage can still be undone. The Jewish settlers can come back, or they can, if settling is their thing, go to the Negev or Galilee in north Israel. Whatever became of Ben-Gurion's idea of settling the Negev desert, to make it fruitful? Of course life there is much harder. From there you can't just hop into a car and drive to a restaurant in Tel Aviv or go to a movie. For most, the settlements are nothing but cheap, comfortable housing close to the city, bedroom towns under army protection. That's not what I call a pioneering spirit, nothing at all like the building of the early days. Some of the settlements are no more than ten minutes from Tel Aviv. What a brave venture into the wilderness! During the day you go to your well-paid job in the city, and at night you go home to a little house you could never afford in the city. Wonderful! Settling the desert, now that's what I call a challenge. The idea of settling your own country doesn't seem to occur to anybody. Political work today means work against the Arabs and less and less work for your own country. At best, the Ethiopians are sent into the desert. All the others are moving out.

I'm also fed up with the Labor Party. The Socialists are afraid of going into opposition. There's no denying that they helped enormously in the building of the country, but now they ought to pull back and let these Likud pols clean up their own mess. But I really shouldn't say all these things about Likud. My husband supports them. Naturally that makes for lively political discussions in our house. On the whole I think that's healthy. It's an antidote to boredom. The two of us see the political situation from different perspectives. But in fact neither of us is very involved politically. We have our own opinions, but it's not an essential part of our personalities. I love my husband neither despite nor because of his politics. That's pretty unimportant.

When I look at my two daughters I nurse the hope that we will be able to help them more than our parents could help us, and that they'll be able to live in a country of which they need not be ashamed.

SIBLINGS:
MIRIAM and DAVID

M: Tell me the truth: when did you last shoot an Arab?

D: I don't remember.

M: And when did you last beat one up?

D: I don't remember that either.

M: But how can you forget beating up a woman?

D: I can.

M: Or hitting a teenager over the head with a nightstick? How can you forget the face?

D: He doesn't have a face.

M: What does he have?

D: He's got two arms and two hands, and a rock in each hand. And between his arms there's a head with a gaping hole out of which he keeps on screaming.

M: And you keep on hitting that hole.

D: Yes.

M: No problem?

D: No problem.

M: How's that possible?

D: I think of Amnon, lying next to me on the ground, his face smeared with blood. Dead. With a hole in his head.

M: And that's when you can hit?

D: Yes, that's when I can hit.

M: And when the Arab, covered with blood, lies next to you on the ground?

D: It doesn't make me feel any better.

M: But you still do it?

D: Yes.

M: But Amnon was a soldier, and the other one is still half a child.

D: A child sent out by his mother to kill me.

M: So you kill in order not to be killed yourself?

D: Yes, something like that.

M: And it makes you feel good, a soldier fighting against children?

D: Who says I feel good?

M: Then why do you do it?

D: I'm not fighting against them; they're fighting against us.

M: They're defending their rights.

D: What rights?

M: It's a question of their country.

D: That's in Jordan. Now they're living on our land, and they're not behaving like guests.

M: But they're here now. Where should they go?

D: I don't care. Best of all, where they came from.

M: Would you drive them out?

D: Yes.

M: Why?

D: They want to destroy us.

M: You want to do the same thing to them what has been done to Jews for centuries.

D: And so?

M: In that case you're no better than our enemies.

D: I don't want to be better. I want to live.

M: You could live with them.

D: No.

M: Why not?

D: I'd always be afraid.

M: Why afraid?

D: For years they've been saying that they want to kill us. They blow up kindergartens; they throw people overboard. And you ask me why I'm afraid? Why aren't you?

M: I trust them.

D: Why, suddenly?

M: I have no other choice.

D: That sounds crazy.

M: It is.

D: You believe somebody who only a short time ago wanted to murder you?

M: Yes.

D: Why? Give me one good reason.

M: I have to. It's my only chance.

D: Who's making you?

M: My intelligence.

D: You think only stupid people are afraid?

M: No. But stupid people *like* to be afraid.

D: And suppose it turns out you made a mistake?

M: It's a risk I have to take.

D: But you'll be dead.

M: Maybe. But I also can't go on living like this.

D: That's your answer to possible suicide?

M: I think the others also want to live.

D: What do you want me to do?

M: Get out of the army.

D: Then others will take over my job.

M: But at least you won't be a part.

D: I always thought I'm also protecting you.

M: No, you're endangering me.

D: How am I standing in your way?

M: I want negotiations and peace.

D: I also want peace, but with an enemy who's lost a war against me.

M: It's a war we cannot win.

D: But we also can't lose.

M: I know. Father fought, and always won.

D: Right!

M: And our enemies lost all their wars.

D: Right!

M: But this time we weren't attacked in our country.

D: But now it's again our country.

M: It's useless. You're so bitter.

D: Right!

M: Why?

D: Too many of my friends are dead.

M: So why add to their number?

D: There'll be still more if I stop fighting.

M: Can you give in? Make concessions?

D: No, it's too late.

M: You don't see any other way?

D: It's a matter of feelings, not of reason.

M: I can't reach your heart?

D: No, it's surrounded by a protective wall. Jewish children blown up by bombs; women, men, shattered skulls of Jewish soldiers—those are images I can't get rid of.

M: David, you're my brother. Don't we have anything in common?

D: Yes, our language, our parents, our country, and also our enemies. But we see them differently.

M: David, I'm afraid.

D: Me too. That's why I'm a soldier.

M: Are you the stronger of us two?

D: No. You are!

M: What makes you think so?

D: You're the braver one.

M: I don't understand you.

D: You want to negotiate with our enemies and you trust them. Your only weapon is your courage and your hope.

M: And given all that, I need you, in case I turn out to be wrong.

LARRY

My parents are Polish Jews who were lucky enough to get out of Europe in the nick of time, in 1940, and come to America. My father had led a colorful life. He was born in a small town in a world I know only from books and movies. In 1925, when he was twelve, he was brought to Israel by his parents. They settled in a Hasidic enclave near Haifa. While still in his teens, he became active in the communist movement. He was arrested and jailed by the British, and he spent two years in prison. He was then around eighteen or nineteen. Immediately after his release the British deported him, and he returned to Poland alone. Years later a former high-ranking intelligence official told me that he had reason to believe that my father may subsequently have been recruited by the Russians to spy on the Nazis. I have no way of knowing whether that's true or not, and I never asked my father, but in view of my informant's credentials I suspect that it's true.

Back in Poland Father suffered the same fate as in Israel, being jailed for his communist activities. I don't know whether it was his political problems or a premonition of the terrible fate awaiting the Jews that made my parents leave Poland for Paris in 1937. But there, too, history caught up with them. This time they just barely managed to get out. The German army was at the gates of Paris when they caught the last train out of there. Then came emigration to the United States. They settled in New York, where I was born in 1951. In 1960 we moved to Los Angeles, and except for two years in San Francisco, I lived there till 1985.

Even though Father, a dyed-in-the wool communist, was an atheist, we still observed the High Holy Days. Family always meant a great deal to him, and these observances strengthened the feeling of family. He also sent me to Hebrew school and I was bar-mitzvahed. But it was a mere formality. It would be wrong to say that I received religious instruction.

Even though they were Polish Jews, my parents generally spoke English at home, not Yiddish. I remember the occasional Yiddish phrase, the way you remember children's nursery rhymes for the rest of your life. But I never learned to speak or even understand Yiddish, let alone read or write it. Within the space of a single generation that language had become lost to us.

All my real friends were Jews, probably because I grew up in a predominantly Jewish neighborhood and went to Hebrew school. I never had anything to do with any Zionist youth group, and I really don't know whether any of my friends or neighbors did. As I said, the Jewish part of my upbringing was purely decorative. At the High Holy Days the food and the presents were the most important part, which probably is the case with children everywhere, whatever their religion.

Israel: all that name meant to me for the first three decades of my life was a small strip of land on a map. I knew absolutely nothing about the country, its geography, history, and culture. Who were Israel's neighbors? What kind of political parties did it have, what were its political goals, how did its people see themselves? Palestinians? Somewhere I suppose I'd heard or read about them, but I had no idea who they were, where they lived, what they were fighting for. I didn't know where the West Bank was. I knew nothing. If someone had asked me who Abraham was I might have answered, a Jew. That about sums it up.

Not until 1984, at the age of thirty-three, did I get the urge to find out more about Israel. What explains this sudden interest? Probably only young people and Americans are apt to act so spontaneously. A good friend of mine was living in Israel, and he wrote me an enthusiastic letter about his life there and also about his job as a TV news editor. Suddenly the idea of going to Israel took hold of me. I had arrived at a point in my life where I was searching for something. I'd done many things: college; after that six or seven years as an actor; then back to college; and at age thirty I got a B.A. in public relations. I hoped to write. The two things I wanted to do most in my life were acting and writing.

Right after getting my degree I got an interesting job as a reporter for a Los Angeles radio station. I stayed for three and a half years, half of that time covering the Olympics. That, of course, was great, being part of all that excitement and enthusiasm, seeing the pride of the winners and the disappointment of the losers up close. But the Olympics ended, and it was back to the old routine. I began to feel restless. I needed a fresh challenge, although I still didn't know what I wanted to do with my life.

That's when my friend's letter arrived. Go to Israel? It had never entered my mind. But now suddenly it began to appeal to me. It set me thinking that spending two years living and writing in Israel might not be such a bad idea, maybe even better than covering the Olympics. And a year after I got that all-important letter I reached the firm decision to go and take a look and maybe write about it. And having reached that decision, I thought I ought to inform myself about the country. However, there wasn't much time. In January 1985, just two months after reading my first book about Israel, I took off. It's fair to say that at the time I still knew next to nothing about what I'd find.

My friend was not my only contact there. I also had some cousins from New York who'd moved to Jerusalem a short time before, as well as relatives I didn't know who'd been living in Israel for years. Suddenly I showed up, a cousin they hadn't seen for ages, a distant relative they'd never met, and the warmth of their welcome was overwhelming. I realized that here was something very special. Perhaps the stuff dished out by the Jewish Agency also played a part, but there's no other way of putting it: I fell in love with that country. Absolutely. It was love.

I had planned on staying around a year or two. Never for a moment did I think that I'd stay any longer, let alone for good. I thought of my trip as more in the nature of an exploration of a new area, after which I'd return home. But it wasn't long before I began to toy with the idea of staying here. I kept on mulling it over. I would be lying if I were to pinpoint any specific moment as the turning point, the one when I reached the sudden decision to stay, never to leave. I don't think that I ever put it in these terms. Rather, it was a sort of provisional decision. And then, a lot of time passed, maybe two years, before I began to think that I might possibly leave again, but not, I told myself, before serving in the military. And I'd set myself still another goal—getting a job on a paper. And I'd found it, my first full-time job, about half a year after my arrival, as an editor at the *New Outlook*. But I didn't stay there for long. Considering that I'd taken part in Peace Now demonstrations, it may seem strange that I quit because I thought the paper too leftist. But it's the truth. I had a great many problems with some of the positions *New Outlook* supported. Now I'm working for the *Jerusalem Post.* The problem I have there is that the *Post* is millions of light-years to the right of me.

I've now been here for five years, and I took out Israeli citizenship two years ago. Last June, four and a half years after coming here, I went into the military. Knowing that I was doing my part made me feel good. It somehow legitimized me as an Israeli.

All this may seem very contradictory, considering my past. Being born in 1951 meant that I grew up in an era of strong antiwar sentiment. I opposed the Vietnam War and joined in all the antiwar demonstrations, and like many of the youthful demonstrators I evaded the draft. Then, in the late seventies, when the problem of the Vietnam veterans became a lively issue in the United States, I began to have second thoughts. I felt guilty. Those veterans had supported and fought in the war while I opposed it, and they had paid for their convictions. I hadn't. It had been so easy just to be against it.

In retrospect, I wish I had acted differently. Of course I'm glad not to have been in Vietnam. I'm still convinced that every casualty there was a tragic waste of human life. My view of that war hasn't changed, but I wish that I and my liberal, demonstrating friends had run the risk of going to jail, or claimed conscientious-objector status and gone to the front as medics. In other words, I wish we had acted instead of taking the easy way out. It's no accident that the antiwar demonstrations stopped as soon as nobody was called up anymore. That's why I've changed my mind about all these things; that's why I am happy to have been in the army here, to have done my part. When I was eighteen I acted according to my beliefs, but now I ask myself, What does an eighteen-year-old know? At eighteen I was just stupid. It was so easy to avoid serving. An eighteen-year-old may think he knows what he's doing, but in fact he doesn't know anything. And I'm sure I was no exception. I said I had my reasons for what I did, but did I really understand what it was all about? I'm not sure.

People are often called upon to make decisions before they're mature enough. Young Israelis voluntarily go to the West Bank. Are these eighteen-year-olds more compliant than their American counterparts? Or more mature? You can't generalize. Ignoramuses and fools are not the exclusive property of any one country, just as young people who act in accordance with what they hold to be right aren't. Still, there's a great difference between the youth of Israel and America. Young Israelis are much more mature, and at the same time often much more childlike. But what truly sets them apart is the reality of being in the midst of things and having to carry a heavy burden. They are growing up in a permanent war zone. The constant threat to the country by its neighbors must inevitably affect the way they think and feel.

With that we have arrived at a crucial point. A year and a half ago I got married and now have a very young son, and as soon as you become a parent you begin to wonder whether Israel is the right place to bring up children. Should my children grow up in a country whose very existence is a thorn in their neighbors' side? Next Sunday I am going to Gaza with my army unit, and nobody can guarantee that my son won't also have to go to Gaza one day. Nobody. Unless something extraordinary, revolutionary, happens in this country, he too will have to go to Gaza. And that worries me.

The future of my child is my greatest concern. Whether to stay, or for the sake of our son try to establish ourselves somewhere else, is a serious question, and we haven't found an answer. In principle I'm against raising children here. The threat of war is too great. And there are other reasons that speak against staying.

My wife is from South Africa, and she doesn't see things the same way. She finds staying here less of a problem. But I also know that she'd be ready to try living somewhere else, though not America. I recently visited there, and dual citizenship or not, I still consider myself an American rather than an Israeli.

Still, I've changed. I wouldn't want to go back to Los Angeles. I no longer like it there. I don't think that I could live in any big American city. A smaller or medium-sized town would be more to my liking, but my wife wouldn't care for that. We've talked about going to South Africa. There's a good chance that we might give it a try. I feel confident that I could get a decent job there and that from a material perspective we'd live as well as here. No question, we're doing well here. We have a beach-front apartment, I have relatives and friends, and my wife likes it here. But those thoughts about the future are unsettling. There's always the question whether to leave or to stay. And like most people here, I complain and I stay.

The other thing that really bothers me is working for a disgusting right-wing paper. That upsets me, even though they don't interfere with what I write. They say dreadful things in their editorials but they don't touch my copy.

Another problem is the language. I don't find it easy. Sure, I manage. I even work in Hebrew, but it still leaves a lot to be desired. I can read the paper and talk to people as long as their conversation isn't too elevated. I can listen to TV and understand the gist of the newscasts, but still, it's a foreign language.

Recently I covered a criminal trial, and that was really difficult. I had a rough idea what was going on, but I missed a great deal. For someone who writes, who likes to read, and who loves the English language it's difficult to live in a country whose language he understands yet hasn't really mastered, which isn't really a part of him. I feel limited. Okay, I don't yet master the language. The question is, will I ever?

This country, Israel, has become a part of me. So many abstract, hard-to-define factors bind me to it. If I were to go to South Africa I'd probably live as well, but I'd never feel at home there. If you live in a country for any length of time—after all, it's almost five years that I've been here—it is natural to look at things more soberly, more realistically than at first. You take off the rose-colored spectacles of the tourist and you begin to see the darker side. And so I also find a lot to criticize here. For example, when I went to South Africa and saw how clean everything was, the civilized way in which people treated each other, at least the whites, I often asked myself, Why can't Israel be like this? The parks were so well-tended and the streets so clean. Israel's messiness must be an eyesore to all Western visitors.

Israel has become a part of me. It probably means more to me than to many others. Still, I'm not an Israeli. That first thrill is gone. I'm attached to the country, and even if I were to leave it would always mean a great deal to me. But love . . . ?

When I first came I lived in Jerusalem, and naturally I went to the Wall and visited all the sacred places. But I was thirty-three, and an atheist at heart. I understand and admire religious Judaism, but I don't feel close to it. Religion is a matter of education, and it wasn't part of mine.

I am an Israeli citizen, I served in the army out of conviction, and I feel closely bound to this country. My Israeli identity means a great deal to me. Yet with all that, I am more of an American than an Israeli. We Israelis all have one thing in common, being conflicted about whether to stay permanently, and if we were to leave, where to go. We're not quite at home in this country, yet we no longer feel we belong to any other. We're forever looking for reasons why it's better here or better there and can't accept the reality of a homeland. And because of our constant wondering what the best place is, we make it harder for ourselves to fully accept this country as our home. However, I live here and nobody knows whether I'll ever go away again. Perhaps one day I'll be living abroad and yearn to come back here.

SIMA

I am a product of the calamitous kibbutz system. Both my parents were the children of well-to-do Eastern European families. My father was nine when he and his mother left for Palestine on the last boat out of Europe before the outbreak of the Second World War. His father stayed in Warsaw and was killed in the ghetto uprising in 1943. Grandmother never got over her terrible loss. She was traumatized, and feeling unable to raise her son on her own, she sent him to a kibbutz, Ganigar, where he still lives. The kibbutzim of that era took in a wide variety of troubled children—from the violent to the orphaned.

My mother was born in Palestine. Her parents came from Bukovina. Her mother still lives in Haifa. Her father was one of nine children of a strictly Orthodox family. He was sent to Frankfurt to the rabbinical seminary, but he didn't stay there long. He broke with his parents, and in the 1920s went off to Palestine. He never got over the breach with his parents. He left them then and he never saw them again. Jews who stayed behind in Europe were lost, his parents among them. Israel is full of older people who are eaten up by guilt because they left their parents behind.

My grandfather worked as a laborer in Haifa. He was so antireligious that my mother, his daughter, was not even allowed to speak of God in his presence. And no holidays were observed in their house. Not until he became a grandfather did he begin to talk about his religious upbringing and to tell us about the great rabbis in his family. He probably felt he couldn't talk to his children about his abrupt, final break with his own parents. His family was wiped out in the Holocaust, and now his hatred of his strict upbringing is all mixed up with feelings of guilt.

In her youth Mother headed a Socialist children's group, and she met my father at one of their seminars. They married, she moved into his kibbutz, and soon afterward my older brother was born. I am their second child. There are four of us altogether.

My older brother and I grew up in the kibbutz before they accepted the family as a social unit. At the age of three months babies were moved to the children's house. In line with the kibbutz's pedagogic guidelines, mothers were allowed to visit and nurse their babies only at specified times.

My brother was far less complicated than I. He didn't mind sleeping away from his parents in a room with three other children. I was terribly afraid of the dark and would keep on waking up throughout the night, calling for the nursemaid on duty. Every room had a microphone, and all this calling out in the dark into an impersonal instrument without knowing who'd come because you didn't know who was on duty haunts me to this day. After waking all the other children with my cries, I'd generally be taken to my parents' room. Once there, I had no problem falling asleep.

I still can't understand what sick idea induced them to have children raised by strange women without special training. We were allowed to visit our parents only between four and seven P.M., except on Fridays, when there were no limits to visiting hours. Everything was organized down to the last detail.

The kibbutz children had an entirely different relationship with their parents than children in normal families. One's own parents were like aunts and uncles whose house you visit. In the short time we spent together we treated each other gingerly and politely: no explosive scenes, no anger, no disappointments, no hostility, but also no real joy. Your emotional life was reduced to not creating any problems.

Mother herself hadn't been raised in a kibbutz, and she felt ambivalent about its pedagogical methods. On the one hand she didn't want to step out of line, and therefore couldn't allow her children to step out of line, while on the other hand she understood my fear of being alone at night and my negative reaction to the constant togetherness with other children. Not until my younger sister was born did she admit how she'd suffered under that system. By the time my sister was born children were allowed to sleep at home, and even during the day mothers could spend time with their babies. Nursing and visiting hours had by then been abolished.

In addition, the political situation was very turbulent. During the Six-Day War we often spent whole nights in the air-raid shelter. Obviously, my night fears were not altogether unreasonable, which probably explains why an exception was made for me, allowing me to sleep at home practically until age ten. And they kept my bed in the children's house though I hardly ever used it.

I envy my two younger sisters for growing up in a real home. Naturally, their relationship with our parents is very different. To me my parents seemed like strangers I visited only at specified times. Yet what cements a family is the daily routine, all those nagging everyday problems.

Beginning at age ten, I often spent weekends with school-friends outside the kibbutz, and when I came back home I had nothing but complaints. Their mothers, I said, were different; they made breakfast for their children, much better than the lousy food we got in the dining hall; they read them bedtime stories and tucked them in. Everything there was better and different. I knew that these complaints caused my mother pain, but I think she was too cowed by the kibbutz system to fight it. I don't believe for a moment that she approved of it.

At age seventeen I had my first boyfriend, my first great love, like the plot of a modern novel. He was a volunteer from Germany. That's all my parents needed. Naturally his father had been in the SS, but he himself was completely estranged from his parents and hardly ever saw them. He was tall, blond, blue-eyed, a real German. Shortly after we met he moved from the youth hostel to the kibbutz's volunteer quarters directly across from the administration building, and I moved in with him, which gave everybody a chance to be an eyewitness to my outrageous behavior.

I enjoyed being the center of this scandal, to cause a stir in this pseudoprogressive kibbutz. Michael, my friend, was working alongside my father in the kibbutz's plastics factory. He was an excellent worker—reliable, industrious, typically German. My father had torn feelings. He had to admit that Michael was an excellent worker, but he couldn't come to terms with our affair. To him Michael was the son of an SS man, not a person in his own right. After all, my grandfather had been killed by the Nazis, and because Grandmother had never gotten over that death, my father had been raised almost like an orphan.

I kept on trying to discuss my relationship with Michael with my father. In the abstract he could understand it. He conceded that there was no connection between what Michael's father had done and Michael himself, but emotionally he couldn't accept it. Our affair lasted about a year, during which time I had graduated from high school and moved to Haifa, where I worked as a leader in the youth movement. The work didn't really interest me, but since all my friends were doing it I went along.

In Haifa I also lived in a commune, but it was not as confining as life in the kibbutz. Those were happy, heady days. Eventually Michael returned to Germany and our affair came to an end. As I said, I wasn't particularly interested in my work. I spent every minute I could in the maternity clinic of the local hospital, having decided some time back to study nursing or midwifery, a choice bringing the additional advantage of housing in the nurses' quarters rather than the kibbutz or in a commune with other students from the kibbutz.

I knew full well that I'd have to learn a profession if I wanted to stand on my own two feet and live outside the kibbutz. As a nursing student I got a deferment from the military. When I finished I went into the army. That was no big deal because I was working in my profession and didn't have to wear a military uniform. I did my work like any nurse in any hospital.

During that time I met my future husband. As a computer expert he had applied for a fellowship in the United States. We married, and I was able to leave the military six months early. Marriage is one way of getting out of military service; another one is to become pregnant and later have an abortion. Rather brutal, but it happens all the time.

The marriage was held in and paid for by the kibbutz. It was a huge affair attended by all the kibbutzniks, almost three hundred of them, as well as a huge number of guests from the outside. I think the kibbutz knew that I was not planning to return, but they did it for my father, an important personage there. In theory, important posts in the kibbutz are supposed to be rotated, but like anywhere else, the people in power hang on. And my father did too. At the moment he is in the United States managing a factory that belongs to the kibbutz.

Soon after our marriage my husband and I spent a year in Washington. He was studying and I went to work in a hospital as a nurse's aide. Before long we discovered that we weren't compatible. In addition, my husband was, let's say, not quite as successful in his studies as we might have wished. He went back to Israel, and I followed soon afterward.

Father still had his mother's apartment in Tel Aviv. After her death he had of course made it available to the kibbutz, and people were always staying there, mostly students. It wouldn't have occurred to Father to let me have the apartment when I was studying nursing. After my divorce, and having made it quite clear that I had no intention of returning to Ganigar, I finally persuaded him to give me the apartment, and a lucky thing, too, because rents in Tel Aviv are very high. Many kibbutzniks who really would like to live in the city on their own return to the kibbutz because they have no other choice. The money the kibbutz gives you when you leave isn't enough for an apartment. And to be quite honest, it's not all that easy to break away because of the advantages the kibbutz offers, like getting all your meals.

I live and work in Tel Aviv, but that doesn't mean that I've become a real city person. I still don't feel at home there. I can't stand the hectic pace, and I'm bothered by the mentality of the city people, their typical unfriendliness.

Actually, I didn't bury the hatchet as far as the kibbutz is concerned until very recently. That is to say, I no longer nurse a grudge against Ganigar. It's like breaking your ties to your parents; once you do, you can stop fighting them. I of course had many friends there and I like to visit on weekends. But it makes me sad to see how all the interesting people are gradually leaving because the kibbutz doesn't meet their intellectual and professional needs. The uninteresting, petty bourgeois who're glad not to have to be on their own are the ones who stay. The kibbutz looks after all their needs, their children, their leisure activities, everything. It's like never having to grow up or being in a cage forever. The only thing that interests these people is the amount of their monthly stipend, and the clothing and jewelry they'll be able to buy with it.

The kind of kibbutz community envisioned by its founders, which I remember from my childhood, no longer exists. It has split up into cliques. Nowadays families spend their evenings in front of the TV. The biggest attraction is their new central video transmitter. Every kibbutz household is connected to it, and it shows movies nonstop from four P.M. to midnight. This explains the waning interest in politics and cultural events. Not that the people in the city are all that different, but they're at least responsible for taking care of their own needs and careers. Today's typical kibbutzniks are living in a world without real problems and worries. And so they create pseudoproblems: who did what with whom, where, when, why, and so forth. Most of my college-trained friends there had to wait years for an interesting job, and there was no guarantee that their professional skills would ever be called on or needed. That's why most of them leave that snug nest to try their wings, to make something of themselves on their own. Still—I know this sounds completely contradictory—I think it's entirely possible that if I were to find the right partner and become pregnant I might return to the kibbutz. Now the kibbutz is a paradise for children.

I've done everything life in the city has to offer. Tel Aviv is like any other big city. It's got jazz clubs and artists and nightlife. For a time I had a boyfriend who was very involved politically—in touch with PLO people, and once he was even arrested. Life with him was exciting, but there came a day when I'd had enough. I went back to nursing, and am now working in a cancer ward. Standing on the sidelines watching the world around me collapse is not my thing. I prefer a hands-on approach to the problems of life.

And the kibbutz? Perhaps it's only a dream, not reality, but the family, an institution they no longer question, is, I think, better off there.

My siblings reflect the changes the kibbutz has undergone. My older brother also left as soon as he got out of the army, took various jobs, traveled, and is now studying mechanical engineering at Haifa. Even though it has taken him a long time to find himself, he always had his feet on the ground. He never chased after money; he is socially aware and he doesn't blame others for his mistakes. We're very similar.

My younger sisters, however, are another story. They like designer labels and expensive things. They seem to resent our parents for living so modestly, for staying in a kibbutz instead of having a house with a swimming pool in an expensive suburb of Tel Aviv. They are no different from the young people in the city, except perhaps for their complete lack of responsibility. The kibbutz is responsible for the way they are, they say, so let it pay.

I simply can't understand that attitude. I always knew that my aspirations were very different from those of many of my friends in the kibbutz. I went my own way, and if I return it will be because I want to. I don't need material help. That's not my aim in life.

AHMED

In 1961, Um-El-Fahem, the Arab town in northern Israel where I was born, was a small village. As its population grew it was elevated to the status of a town. But otherwise nothing has changed. Everything still looks the way it did a hundred years ago. Its sanitation and public institutions—kindergartens, schools, and so forth—are the same as they were when I was born. There's no sewer system, no hospital, no high school.

Mine is a typical middle-class Arab family. My father is a civil servant working for the Ministry of the Interior; my mother is a housewife. I am the oldest of eleven children. All of us either went to or still are in high school, and all of us were top students. Our parents put great store in education. They wanted us to have the opportunities they didn't have. When they were young they couldn't get an education because of the political situation. They came of age during the turbulent days of the founding of the state. Jordan was cut off, and with it the hinterland.

I went to elementary school in our village. After that, even though I'm a Muslim, I was sent to a Christian-Orthodox boarding school in Haifa, supposedly one of the best around. Arabs of all religious persuasions—Christians, Muslims, and Druse—went there. Almost all the teachers in that school were Communists.

The majority of Israel's Communist Party is made up of Arabs, and until recently they controlled Um-El-Fahem. They'd always been seen as the party of the underprivileged. But in the past few years the local population switched allegiance. Now the town is governed by a new religious party. I also voted for it. The media have given a completely distorted picture, making it seem as though Khomeini had come here in person. They call us Little Iran in the middle of Israel. Our religious fervor makes them uncomfortable.

Actually, the real reason for the change is that the Communist Party bosses looked out for themselves and didn't do anything for the people. The election was more of a protest vote against the governing group for not having done anything for decades. The religious party now in power is young, energetic, and incorruptible. It is a new movement, in some respects similar to the Greens of Western Europe. The new mayor, for instance, comes of a well-to-do family and has donated his salary to the general fund.

In elementary school the language of instruction was Arabic. In the third grade we began studying Hebrew, and in the fifth, English. Our curriculum was similar to that of the Jewish schools. We read the same poems and stories, and the country's history was taught from the Jewish perspective. Neither Arab culture nor our own history was part of our education. It's an odd situation: we're not strangers here, we grow up among our own kind, but our schools unfortunately don't teach the culture of our own people. Bialik was my favorite poet, mainly because I knew hardly any of the Arab poets and writers. Literature and poetry have remained my overriding passion. I write poetry. I'm somewhat of a romantic, and I'm more interested in art than in politics. My schooling was like that of any other Israeli. I belonged to the Boy Scouts, and on Independence Day we decorated our school with flags and held contests, and our parents prepared a buffet. The high point of the celebration was the address by the visiting education minister. I still remember his telling us that we too were part of this country, and that we won our independence when the British withdrew in 1948. I never questioned that, and no one ever told me that this was a highly dubious contention.

My parents were still very young when the State of Israel was founded. Because of the turmoil in 1948, Father was unable to finish school, and so he became an office worker. Mother came from one of the wealthiest families here, and for a long time they opposed her marrying my father. She was engaged to Father for four years before they got permission to marry. Marriage between people of such different social backgrounds is still rare and is looked at askance.

After graduating from high school I applied for admission to the medical school of Tel Aviv University. Despite my excellent grades I was turned down. This was my first experience with our so-called equal rights and the liberation extolled by the minister. Arabs and Druse were subject to an admissions quota, and once the maximum was reached that was that. I could have majored in biology and switched after a year. But I was too impatient. Father suggested that I go to Rumania to study. I have a cousin there who is a doctor. So I went to Bucharest. There my situation as an Arab Israeli was totally bizarre, almost grotesque.

Those oh-so-progressive Communist Rumanians don't like Arabs. They consider them primitives unfamiliar with Western customs; also, many of the criminals in Rumania were Arabs. But as soon as they heard I was an Israeli, people became extremely friendly. Other Arabs had a much harder time. On the other hand, I had hardly any contact with the handful of Jewish Israelis there. We'd greet each other if we happened to meet, but that was all. It was like a reflection of my torn situation: enjoying the advantages of the Israelis but being shunned by them, yet suffering none of the disadvantages of the Arabs.

My discussions with Jordanian students were highly interesting. They were under the impression that all Israeli Arabs voluntarily or involuntarily had converted to Judaism and had shed all traces of Arab identity. The very fact that I was more fluent in Arabic than in any other language confused them. They were convinced that Arabic was forbidden in Israel, and the mere fact that someone like me existed puzzled them.

I found I couldn't discuss politics with them because I had grown up with Israeli historiography and wasn't sure whether something like a Palestinian nation even existed prior to 1948. At times I had the feeling that they and I weren't even talking about the same thing, that we were discussing two different conflicts in two different countries. Even though I was an Arab I saw everything from the Israeli perspective and interpreted different historical facts differently from the Jordanians.

My parents never were critical of Israel or Jews, and I never heard them utter a bad word. Given my background I tended to believe Israeli history texts, and I thought that what the Jordanians were telling me was nothing but PLO propaganda.

Eighteen months ago, having completed my medical studies, I returned to Israel. I'm working in the municipal hospital of Tel Aviv. Until my return from Rumania I'd had hardly any dealings with Jewish Israelis. I was a little afraid before I began to work here, because I'd heard many disconcerting stories about how the Jews treat us, that they look down on us, exploit us, assign us to the most menial tasks.

I've had both good and bad experiences, and I've discovered that there's no logic to discrimination and prejudice. As an Arab in Rumania I met with even more rejection than here, but as an Israeli I had advantages. Here it's the other way round, although everybody has been very polite. Perhaps they even treated me better than the Jewish doctors who started together with me. The atmosphere was almost too friendly, as though they were afraid of discriminating against me. The chief resident would often let me go home after night duty while he made others stay. In the time I've been here I can't remember hearing a single hostile word. It's also possible that I don't want to hear any. But as I told you, I'm not a political person, and I also don't judge people by their politics but by the way they behave toward me. I look at a person's face and listen to his tone of voice, not necessarily to what he's saying. It's all a matter of feeling, of intuition. In my dealings with Jews I try to feel them out, to find out whether there is antipathy or not. Nothing is put into words.

Six months ago I was transferred to another clinic. In introducing myself to the head doctor I told him that I had only one request, to be treated the same as all the others. This man is religious and probably a rightist politically, and I felt a little uneasy about the reassignment. But he has always behaved correctly. As a doctor he treats me the same as his Jewish colleagues.

Yet I can't deny that discrimination has affected my life and career. Having studied in Rumania, I am at a qualitative disadvantage. Most of my colleagues studied either in Israel or in a Western country. The medical training I received is not on the same level. I was unfamiliar with the advanced technical equipment and machinery here, but I'm beginning to catch up.

In addition, as an Arab doctor you always have the feeling of merely being tolerated. If there were enough Jewish doctors they'd probably send us home. The other problem is the patients. Some don't want to be treated by me, don't trust me, or ask for a second opinion, and some, though by no means most, refuse to have me touch them at all. Somehow it's impossible to relax; you're never judged on your merits.

I and my wife and child live in Um-El-Fahem, and I commute to the clinic in Tel Aviv. Not only do we feel at home in our little town (my wife also grew up here), but we couldn't possibly afford an apartment in Tel Aviv. I also help support my parents and siblings because Father's salary and the little bit Mother makes with her dressmaking isn't enough to pay for the children's education, and until all of them are self-supporting I can't even afford a car. Sometimes I feel a little angry, but I know why I've assumed this burden. As a minority we are lost without an education. If we want to get ahead we must acquire professional skills.

Occasionally it's advisable to keep your Arab identity secret, and since I dress in Western clothes I can do it. Since the disorders everything has become much more difficult. Normal coexistence is a thing of the past; still, I can't live in constant conflict with those around me. And the problems keep multiplying.

Once in Hadeira I took a group taxi to Tel Aviv and began talking Arabic with the driver, whereupon all the other passengers got out. Two Arabs in the same spot was more than they could handle. Ever since then I pretend not to understand Arabic; I prefer avoiding unpleasantness to confrontation.

Only once did I get involved in a dispute. It was a matter of principle. After finishing high school I worked in a paper factory to make money for my trip to Rumania. The foreman was an Iraqi Jew. I make a point of this, because an Ashkenazi would never have behaved the way he did. Our difficulties are always with Jews from Arab countries. This man knew that I was planning to study medicine, and that apparently didn't sit well with him. In his eyes Arabs were nothing but primitive workhorses, so why send them to school? Once, at the end of the day, he called me away from a group of Jewish and Arab workers, and in front of all of them ordered me to sweep the yard. I refused and told him that he had others to do this work, but if this was part of the job he should give me a helper from among the Jewish workers. When he repeated his order and I again refused, he fired me on the spot. There was nothing I could do. What had really gotten to me was that he had insulted me in front of the others. And nobody intervened, not the Jews and not the Arabs.

On the whole, I try to avoid all political discussions, above all in the hospital. Still, you can't help becoming involved, whether you want to or not. It's as though every Arab is held accountable for all. Once, some Arab hospital workers hoisted a PLO flag, a pointless gesture. They were promptly arrested. Next morning a nurse I'd been friendly with said to me, "You know what's going to happen to the terrorists who put up the PLO flag, don't you?" And as she spoke she smiled almost provocatively. I was an Arab, and so I belonged among the terrorists. I pretended not to hear and left the room. Later, when she and I were alone in the examination room, I talked to her calmly about the incident, and she in turn responded calmly. Of course she knew that I had nothing to do with this whole affair.

I don't intend to leave my town and move to Tel Aviv. I also can't imagine where and how I and my family could live here among all Jewish neighbors, and perhaps even among a Jewish circle of friends. We might possibly live in Jaffa, which has an Arab infrastructure. For the children it would certainly be easier to go to school with Arab children. Also, I don't know where my wife could find a job here. She is a bookkeeper, but who here would hire an Arab bookkeeper? We doctors also don't have such an easy time getting hospital jobs; they try to persuade us to go into private practice in our hometowns. Yet on the whole, I don't think that everything here is bad. There are countries in which minorities have a really lousy time. And finally, given my academic background, I have a better chance of getting elected to parliament than the average Israeli.

If a Palestinian state were to come into being I wouldn't want to move there, for two reasons. First, my home is here in Israel; my family, relatives, and friends live here. But the second and equally important reason is my belief that a Palestinian state wouldn't be democratic. I grew up in a democratic state, and alone the fact that I'm able to have this conversation with you and speak my mind is an advantage I'm not ready to give up.

Jews seem to look on us Arabs as a single group, regardless of where we live, whether Um-El-Fahem or Gaza or Nablus. But that's not true. I have even less contact with Arabs in the territories than with Jewish Israelis. It's strange, Jews complain about the way they are seen, but they make the same mistake with us. They get angry when they are referred to collectively as "the Jews," but they talk about "the Arabs." On the other hand, I have a problem with the kind words of many Europeans. For them, we're the "oppressed Arabs." All those clichés and crude generalizations. None of these unwelcome "friends" takes the trouble to differentiate among us. I also don't feel like being used as a weapon in the battle against Israel or the Jews. I belong to a more or less protected minority in this country, while an Arab from Gaza belongs to a violently oppressed majority in the occupied territories. There's a world of difference between the two.

I was raised in a Western culture, and that naturally has left its mark. By contrast, someone from Nablus or Gaza is as far removed from Western culture today as before the Six-Day War. The only things that unite us are religion and food. I can feel it in my place of work. Like my father, I'm not particularly religious. When I was in Rumania, for example, I drank alcohol. But I'm traditional, and so I fast at Ramadan, even when I'm working.

Something happened once that brought my inner conflict to the fore. One evening as I was about to start my duty rounds, I went to the hospital canteen to grab a bite. One of the nurses said she felt sorry that at the end of my fast I wasn't able to get a little more and better food. She suggested that I go to the room of the housecleaning staff where the Arab workers were having their meal. She thought they'd most certainly be eating a far better meal than the bread and yogurt served at the canteen. I told her that I didn't know the people there and couldn't just invite myself simply because we were of the same religion. I felt defensive because I assumed that to her I was just another Arab. A moment later one of those workers—most of them are Arabs from the territories—came over and invited me to share their meal. The food wasn't exactly like Mother's, but it was wonderful to sit down with fellow Muslims to an Arab meal instead of to that awful yogurt. The next day one of the workers came to see me and said that the nurse who had felt sorry for me had suggested that they invite me to a decent supper. Those are the sort of incidents that transcend all prejudice.

GIL

You see, on the one hand I can accept having to serve in this country, having to sacrifice myself, but on the other, it's not my fault that I was born an Israeli. I don't see why, just because I was born an Israeli and a Jew, I have to stay here or why I am supposed to feel guilty if I should decide to leave. Who says so, who's asking it of me? Should I feel bad if I, like other young people, want to see the world, to learn something, to make money? Should I feel bad for no longer doing my annual stint in the reserves? For not risking my life? I am a human being before I am a Jew and an Israeli citizen. I want my freedom, and if I believe that I'll be better off somewhere else, I'd like to be able to leave Israel without having to feel guilty. I also don't see why I have to pay such high taxes. The minute my income goes up the state takes half of it away, mostly to pay for the army. Why? Who is this state anyway?

I didn't always have so many misgivings, but too much has happened to this country, and also to me and my family. When I went into the army I volunteered for the Golani, the elite infantry division every young male Israeli wants to serve in. Their reputation is second only to the air force's. Of course, being a pilot is almost like being a movie star. But it's also not all that easy to become a Golani. They don't take you if you are an only child, and you must have a test score of 97 out of a possible 100. The training takes months, and you need your parents' permission. As a ground force the Golanis are always out in front.

But everything went wrong for me. They didn't take me, for family reasons. It was necessary for me to be stationed close to home. So I left them to train as a medic in one of the big camps near Tel Aviv.

Our family was hit by the tragedy of war. One of my brothers returned from the war in Lebanon with a serious head injury from which he never fully recovered. He needs constant supervision. He might be all right for weeks at a time, completely normal, and then suddenly something happens without warning and he becomes like a helpless child, or worse still, like a wild animal doing bizarre, unpredictable things.

This is not simply like having someone at home in need of constant care. It is a sickness that destroys the entire family. It spares none of us. And why? What did my brother do to deserve this kind of punishment? And the rest of the family? That's why I want to get out of here. Can you understand? All I want is just to get out of here.

Freedom is a wonderful thing. I know it sounds simple, but I didn't realize how important personal freedom is until I went abroad for the first time. I took off as soon as I got out of the army, and spent a year in America and Europe. Perhaps I shouldn't have, because after what I saw there I find life here even more difficult. The people over there live in freedom.

There's also a great difference between the concept of democracy here and in other Western countries. Actually we don't have real democracy here. What kind of independence is it that the state celebrates on Independence Day? You can't call either the individual citizen or the state, which is dependent on America, truly independent. But what bothers me most of all is the interference of the state in the private sphere of the citizens, something that was brought home to me when I went into business on my own and had to register with the tax authorities. You can't imagine how complicated everything is here. In addition, I have to make a monthly payment into my personal pension fund. The state tells you that this is a good arrangement, that they are setting up savings for your pension. That's nice of them, but suppose I don't want it and would rather spend my money on other things? Suppose I starve when I'm old? Why does the state force me to be happy? Big Brother, always looking after us, always somebody who means well, who reminds you that what's at stake here is not just any old country but Israel.

If you want to know the truth, the system here in Israel is a scandal. Take the military, for instance. Not enough that I served for three years. If I serve for six weeks a year in the reserves between now and age fifty-six, I will have given the state an additional eight years. But even that's not enough. Those who don't pay into the pension fund get nothing from the state, even though they've risked their lives.

I'm going to find myself a spot in the world that is more democratic, that allows the individual greater freedom. I have no interest in trying to change things here. It's like Don Quixote and the windmills.

What I want above all is to do what's best for me, for once to think of myself and not of the state or the Jews. I'm not one of those eager to die for this country. But it's almost impossible here to preserve your individuality.

Everything is public; there is no distance between you and your surroundings.

How long can an Israeli stand it without listening to the news? Every half hour they turn on their radios, waiting to hear the news. People here are completely dependent on what's happening; they aren't allowed to develop in peace or withdraw into themselves. Nowhere else in the world do people read as many papers as here, or know all about the politicians and what they said yesterday and what they're going to do tomorrow. Under these conditions it's impossible to concentrate on yourself. In Europe and America people seem to be much more relaxed, not so nervous. When I was abroad I stayed with friends who didn't listen to the news for days on end, who weren't afraid they'd missed something if they didn't see the papers. There's not the kind of hysteria you find here.

Everybody here talks about politics, about whether you're for or against negotiations, what the Americans said yesterday and what they said this morning, whether the French are for or against us. Every conversation among friends sooner or later turns to politics; political cabarets are the best things on TV; every other joke is political. I can't think of a single nonpolitical joke. Everything revolves around the magic word "security." If you were to eliminate it from the language people would be struck dumb. They don't have a personal vision of their future; European-style individuality isn't in demand. They seem to think that they should be admired and rewarded merely for living in a Jewish state. They expect somebody somewhere to come up with money to help them out. After all, the world is full of rich people. Individual initiative—who needs it?

The young people here are no better than the old ones. Many of my friends don't agree with me. They're just like all the other Israelis. They accept the existing situation and try to make the best of it. Getting by is their motto. But I'm not willing to accept things as they are. I'm not ready to serve in the army for even one more day. I refuse to let the fact that I was born an Israeli commit me to a cause I'm not convinced of.

I'm of course troubled by our being surrounded by hostile states. It would be nice to live in peace. I often think how nice it would be to go to Amman or Damascus for a weekend, to live in a decent hotel, to eat well. True, I can go to Cairo. Sounds nice, but every time you leave the country you have to get permission from the military authorities, and if you're scheduled for reserve duty in the near future they don't grant it. In addition, you have to pay a departure tax. That's Israeli democracy for you!

Everything is a struggle here; nothing moves normally, quietly, smoothly. Teachers make so little that they can't even afford an apartment, and the same holds true for doctors. So what do they do? They take extra jobs, while regular army personnel can take early retirement at age forty-five. And in addition they get a big bonus. The top officers really come into their own when there's a war; that's when they feel important, when they're in combat, defending themselves. That's how they get their orgasms.

I don't feel that I owe anybody anything. I gave the military three years of my life, perhaps my three best years. And what did I get? A maimed brother. They used him and then they shipped him back to us, unfortunately a little bit frayed around the edges.

You can't believe the sort of thing the military does to you. A good friend of mine committed suicide because he couldn't cut it in the army. And he was full of good intentions and ambition when he went in. His father was a big shot in the military, and my friend also wanted to rise and serve the state. But he couldn't take the military routine, those stupid drill masters who belittle you. He landed in the brig because of some minor incident, and he killed himself. He wrote it in a letter, that's how I know about it. Nobody else does. All his father talks about is his own heroism. And then he had a son, a failure, sitting in a military prison.

Nobody ever talks about the young people in the army who kill themselves. Every soldier killed by an Arab is a hero, but no one ever talks about those driven to suicide by their own people. And there are more of them than victims of the intifada. If this boy hadn't had to go into the army who knows what he might have accomplished? But the military ground him down. And those who've already served their term also can never return to full civilian life. Every year you get called back. Israel actually doesn't have any real civilians anymore.

If I were to go abroad and, let's say, a war broke out, I would probably volunteer. I'm ready to help in an emergency. Of course I care about the survival of this state. I want it to survive, but not have it take its toll of me every day of my life.

I admire Israel's past, the remarkable things that were accomplished in such a brief time. But not only was that another time, it was also an entirely different generation. The early accomplishments, the enthusiasm, the communal spirit, all that is gone forever. These are different times. We young ones want to live, and live well. The state is no longer so important to us. We ask ourselves, Why can't we be as well off as other young people in other countries? My parents are of a different generation. They fled from Iraq in 1951 and came here, at a time when Jews were being persecuted in Iraq. They escaped with forged papers. When they first got here they lived in a series of refugee

camps, in crowded, vermin-infested barracks. After a year
they were given a piece of land in an agricultural commune,
but misfortune continued to pursue them. There were constant problems with Arab neighbors who destroyed their
crop and thus the basis of their existence. And that wasn't
even the worst of what they did to them.

They left the commune, and on their own, without the
help of the immigration authorities, they moved to Jerusalem. Until he retired my father was a construction worker
and my mother took care of her ten children. I'm the youngest. My parents are very old-fashioned, simple people. And
they also have very little interest in politics. What was
always important to Mother was having a clean house,
getting the children ready for school, shopping for food,
and cooking for us. Her political horizon is limited to
cursing out the finance minister when the price of food
goes up.

My relationship to my father is almost nil. Except for
"Good morning" and "How are you?" we hardly ever
speak to each other. Father still lives in the belief that when
children grow up they should learn a trade and start a
family. His idea of a normal life is completely alien to me.
We had a little talk before I went abroad. He couldn't
understand why I worked at all those odd jobs only to
throw away all that money on a trip. He would have
wanted me to use my savings to buy a business or an
apartment. He also doesn't understand people who go to
college. Why all that learning if good money can be made
as a carpenter or running a vegetable stand?

My parents have no understanding of the idea of freedom. As far as they are concerned they became free the
day they left Iraq. They have no concept of personal freedom. They don't understand it, while I yearn for it. After
they escaped from Iraq, Israel became their paradise. But

unlike them, I didn't come out of a prison. I have a different notion of freedom.

My parents are like most Israelis who have never been abroad. They are Zionists and love Israel largely because that's all they know. Many of those people dig in here because they're afraid of the big world outside. Take my brother-in-law and my sister. They've never been outside Israel. Now my brother-in-law, a research physician, has received a two-year study grant in the United States. Of course they'll go, but they are afraid that they might not return and in a manner of speaking throw all the ideals of their youth overboard. Their conscience is bothering them, and they haven't even left yet.

My sister was in the army when the Six-Day War broke out. She volunteered for an additional year, and afterward joined a group that founded a kibbutz. A true Zionist, she is suffering pangs of conscience for leaving her home. She thinks it's like a betrayal.

Most of the young people going into the army want to join a combat group. So did I. We're a country that turns its brutal fighters into heroes and role models, and so naturally every young soldier wants to show his stuff. If he can capture a terrorist he becomes a hero, and for about a month afterward he's in seventh heaven.

But how about the ones who serve in the territories? There they have to fight against civilians. One of my brothers was an officer in the war in Lebanon. He is a dedicated soldier, no doubt about it. But after his most recent reserve tour of duty he saw things that changed his attitude completely. His belief in the brave Israeli army is gone. He cannot forget some of the things he saw.

Once his unit was dispatched to an Arab village to get the people to remove the PLO flags from their roofs and to find out who had put them up in the first place. They came to one such house. In front of it sat an elderly man, three young children, and a woman. They were eating. The soldiers went into the garden and asked the man who had put up the flag. No answer. They asked again. Again no answer, whereupon the table with the food came flying through the garden. The children started to cry hysterically and hid behind the man. The soldiers began to hit and kick him until he collapsed, bleeding. At that, the woman turned on the soldiers. She too was beaten until she collapsed. The children ran away as fast as they could, and an Israeli soldier took down the flag.

My brother, who was in charge of the group, suddenly thought to himself how terrible and senseless all this was. The man can't tell us who hoisted the flag out of fear of being killed for his betrayal, and we bloody him and the woman in front of the children because he won't talk, and then we take the flag down ourselves. And tomorrow another one will go up in its place. The only result of this entire affair is the probable birth of three future terrorists. And so my brother has changed his opinion completely. He used to be a right-winger who believed that the Arabs must not be shown leniency because they were out to destroy us. Not anymore. Now he's in favor of giving up the territories, of negotiations with the Palestinians, the PLO. Not that he has suddenly developed love for the PLO, but he is convinced that the continued oppression only increases resistance. The revolt of the Palestinians cannot be broken by force. Only negotiations will bring us the result whose importance far outweighs the idea of which of the two is the stronger—namely, peace.

I still don't like the Arabs. It is difficult to rid oneself of old ideas. The prejudicial notion of the Arabs as cruel, two-faced, untrustworthy, out to kill the Jews, is deeply embedded. However, I must accept their right to their own state. My political views have also undergone a change in the course of the intifada. I too used to think that being strong was the most important thing, and I didn't accept the Palestinians' right to self-determination.

I've been sitting here talking to you for hours about the importance of personal freedom for myself, so how can I deny it to others?

TALI

I had a wonderful childhood. We lived in Jaffa until I was
twelve, and my friends came from various backgrounds.
One was a Christian Arab, the family of another were
Orthodox Jews. I'm convinced that this mixture of early
childhood friends has colored my life. I myself come of a
mixed family—a Sephardic mother and an Ashkenazi father. My friends used to tell me that they envied me. For
a long time I didn't know what they meant.

Jaffa is a beautiful city. On one side there's the ocean
and on the other green fields. It's a wonderful place to
grow up in, full of scents and colors. In the army my parents
had belonged to the same Nahal, the youth group that
combines military service with work in a kibbutz, and after
finishing their stint their group settled down together. I
was brought up in great freedom, like in a kibbutz.

My mother was born in Israel. Her family has been here
for seven generations. Father came here in 1948 from Bes-
sarabia. I can still remember the day the Six-Day War broke
out. I was out walking when suddenly I saw people begin
to run. I became afraid and also started to run, I don't
remember where to, but everybody was running someplace.

And then my father was suddenly gone, and when he returned after a week he had grown a beard. I didn't rec-
ognize him; he looked like a stranger.

I was then going to school, and what struck me was that
one day the streets were crowded and the next day no
people were to be seen. For us kids school continued normally, but we sensed that something was wrong. A dark
cloud seemed to be coming closer and closer. We only heard
fragments of conversations, about someone missing who
wasn't expected to return, and someone else killed in action. I had nightmares. We weren't allowed to turn on the
light after dark, and the grown-ups were glued to the radio
listening to the news.

Once it was over questions began to be asked. We in
school also talked about it a lot. Ever since then the army
and people's attitudes toward it have become one of the
most discussed issues here. I catch myself asking people I
meet where they had served, what they had done while in
the army, whether they knew so and so. Those three years
in the army leave an indelible mark on every Israeli. In
most other countries young people have finished college
by the time our higher education begins.

Like my parents I was in Nahal. Our group wanted to
stay together, and we were sent to Kibbutz Elot. I was glad
to find that things there weren't so rigidly military. I spent
eight months at the kibbutz, and after that came basic
training. There men and women were initially separated;
after six months we were reunited. We were assigned to
setting up a camp for civilians, the kind of work Nahal is
frequently called on to do. This particular camp was near
the Dead Sea. All we found were some huts, a communal
shower, and a kitchen full of sand. The marshy soil there
was not particularly fertile. After a rain you found yourself
knee-deep in mud. We tried to plant some grass around

the huts, but that wasn't very successful. Then we tried growing watermelons. After half a year we'd made some progress. The place had become a little more green and a little more habitable. When the settlers began to arrive we were sent back to Kibbutz Elot. Having shown how good a job we could do, our group was sent to some of the worst places to prepare them for settlers. I was the group secretary, something like a mini-president. What I liked best were the military exercises. After so many wars, exercising while holding a weapon seemed entirely normal. I learned how to use a weapon, but I never had to aim it at another human being.

I was so enthusiastic over the atmosphere in the kibbutz that I stayed on longer than I had to. Eleven of us out of the original fifty stayed on. After leaving I enrolled in the drama department at the university; I graduated four years later. During those four years I supplemented my income by working as a cleaning woman. The work was hard, but I made a lot of money. But the really hard times began after my graduation. It's almost impossible to make a living as an actor. The private theaters pay per performance, the state-run pay a monthly wage. Neither is enough to live on.

Tel Aviv is Israel's liveliest city. I don't want to live in Jerusalem. Life there is so different, so placid and boring. And they don't have any acting studios. The intifada has politicized everything, including my profession. Except for the classics there's hardly a play that doesn't deal with the current situation. We're actors and we do live in the present. At one time I and one of my best friends were in a play about the Palestinian uprising. After it closed my friend was called up, and in a demonstration he was hit by a rock and killed. I still can't get over it. Every time I hear about an Israeli being killed I feel as though it was my dearest friend. Everything happens so quickly here. One day you're appearing in a play, the next day you're called up, and the day after you're dead, maybe after having acted the part of a victim only two days before. None of us chose to become soldiers, least of all my friend who was killed.

I've appeared in plays with a mixed Jewish-Arab cast, and sometimes our roles call on us to fight each other. That's when we try to understand what is really happening out there, to put ourselves in the others' shoes. Once we exchanged roles and tried to play the others, and that too seemed to make sense. During one of our rehearsals one of the actors got so upset that he broke down and cried. After we calmed him down he told us that his brother had been missing for two days. I like appearing in classics. Modern plays don't always offer the same opportunity to act, really act, to grow into a part.

I was once in a film with a mixed Jewish-Arab cast which was never shown. Called *Wedding in Galilee*, it was a highly political picture made specifically for a film festival. Working together with Arab actors naturally brought us closer. After spending all day in front of the camera, we couldn't just forget it all at the end of the day and pretend it didn't mean anything and relax and have fun. We became so involved in the plot that we'd sit together for hours and talk about it.

One of the scenes was filmed in an Arab village near Jerusalem. All the actors, including the Arabs, were in Israeli uniforms. When the local population saw us they began to sing the Palestinian anthem, and their faces were full of hate. Some of the camera crew were Arabs. They didn't know what to do, and so they kept their mouths shut and didn't identify themselves. Later we all took a bus back to the city, and over the radio came news of a terror attack, with fatalities on both sides. We listened to the news together; it was a touchy situation. All of us were sad, probably only because of our own dead. Nobody spoke a word for the rest of the trip. In silence and pain we separated, the Arabs and the Jews. With one stroke we had turned into strangers, even though we'd been working together for weeks.

Obviously my profession is part of the reality here. And as long as there are conflicts, plays will be written about them, a fact of life that doesn't make me feel elated, but it is a challenge.

RENÉ

I didn't come to Israel until 1969, when I was sixteen. I was born in Morocco. My father had worked for the French army, and in 1956, after Morocco became independent, he worked for the Moroccan army. He may well have been the only Jew there. We lived in Meknes, which did have a Jewish community, but because Father had to work Fridays and Saturdays we weren't part of it. Our only social contacts were with other army employees.

Mother came of a very traditional Jewish family, although nothing like the Orthodox Ashkenazim here in Israel. Moroccans aren't as rigid and strict. Theirs is rather a warm, folkloristic Judaism.

When I was eight Father was transferred to Casablanca, and there I attended a private Jewish high school. We were nine children, and all of us were in private schools. That's where I first heard of Israel. Up to then we were just Moroccans of the Jewish faith. Not until the Six-Day War did the situation become more complicated. Morocco was involved in the war with Israel, and when Israel won we felt very proud. It was like a personal victory, even though we considered ourselves Moroccans first.

That war threw me into utter confusion. Jews were beginning to leave Morocco. Friends and neighbors seemed
to disappear overnight. At school we were asked to write
a poem about Israel. In my poem I accused Israel of taking
my friends away. I called Israel a thief of my pals. It seems
to have been a touching poem because the teacher read it
to the class. I didn't understand why all these people
wanted to go to Israel. Men were coming from Israel who
tried to persuade us to leave, but it was all very hush-hush.
The Moroccan government wasn't supposed to know
about it.

My school wasn't Zionist. Most of the kids were proud
Moroccans and not particularly interested in Israel. And
so those men tried to work on our parents. They had a
talk with my parents and managed to convince them of
the advantages of letting us go. However, the principal of
our school dissuaded them. But not long after that I broke
my arm in the gym and had to stay home for three months.
That's when I also had occasion to listen to the arguments
of these men, and soon they convinced us that we'd be
better off in Israel.

Once we'd made the decision to go everything went very
quickly. One day my siblings and I together with three
hundred others were flown to Marseille and brought to a
camp of the Youth Aliyah. Every evening we watched movies about Israel. It looked like paradise on earth: fraternity,
equality, democracy, and pioneering spirit. We couldn't
wait to see it with our own eyes.

When we finally got there we were sent to a religious
boarding school near Haifa. Nobody there paid any attention to me when I tried to tell them that I came from a
nonreligious home. The school was part of an agricultural
youth village, and our day was divided equally between
work and study.

I arrived at the school carrying a suitcase with three suits in addition to the one I was wearing. How were we to know that all we needed here were shorts and sandals? My suits looked completely out of place. The village itself was just rows of cabins along dusty roads. I shared a room with four others who weren't exactly thrilled to see me. They put my mattress in the middle of the room, and that's where I slept. I had come to the Holy Land from an upper-class Moroccan household and an elite school, wearing a suit, a freshly laundered white shirt, a tie, and polished shoes, to this primitive place where the boys perched on tractors and ran around in worn pants. Socks were unheard of. It was terrible.

I was wandering through a haze. I didn't speak Hebrew and nobody there spoke French. The first six months I sat in class not understanding a word. After two months, my sister, who went to school in the same village, asked to be sent back to Morocco. They transferred her to a nicer village, and so she stayed. I was beside myself and I cried a lot. All I wanted was to leave. Worst of all was my loneliness. For the holidays the other children all went home to their parents while I sat around all by myself.

The camp leaders tried to tell me that returning to Morocco was not possible. I didn't know what to do, but eventually I began to adjust. I learned the language and managed to graduate with fairly decent grades. But learning a new language was not all I had to do. I had to erase my French cultural background. By the time my parents arrived a year later I had become an Israeli. I refused to speak French with them and sneered at them for clinging to their bourgeois ways. They tried to live like Moroccans, while I had gone native. At their house it was still Casablanca.

I was called into the army and had no trouble adjusting

there. Nothing seemed to bother me anymore. By acquiring a new culture, a new language, a new way of dressing, I had become a changed person. In the army I met other Israelis, not recent immigrants, but people who had lived here for a long time. They commented on my French accent, and suddenly my Oriental background became an issue. We had discussions about the difference between the Ashkenazim and Sephardim. Again I found myself in a new situation. Later, at the university I heard students talk about the discrimination against the Sephardim, and this once more was something new. People who immigrate to this country are constantly confronted with something new.

The first year at the university was yet another shock. I had been taken out of a country because as a Jew there I was part of an endangered species. Israel was supposed to become the country of my ideals, my Jewish ideals. But then I found out that in this land of the Jews I belonged to an inferior group—the Orientals.

As the son of an educated upper-middle-class Moroccan family and with my French cultural background I considered myself superior to the peasants from Poland and Rumania. None of that mattered. I was the primitive Oriental. And now, despite my Harvard M.A., people still seem surprised that I've come as far as I have. I contradict all the statistics and all their prejudicial notions about Moroccans, those alleged failures in school and in life.

Four of my siblings live abroad, and two more are about to leave, which shouldn't come as a surprise. The fact that we were unable to integrate here is a testimonial to the failure of the Israeli dream. It pains me having to watch our family fall apart, with branch after branch breaking away, not to mention the potential that's being lost to the country. My brothers and sisters in Europe are all highly successful. They were given a chance to show what they could do and they took advantage of the opportunities offered.

For my parents it is also not easy. Only two of their grandchildren live here in Israel. My father was a respected citizen in Morocco, and here he is nobody, an outsider. He still speaks French at home, and all his friends are from his old world. He can't even read his son's articles in the newspaper.

While I was at the university Likud came to power. That was 1977. This political turnaround was the revenge for the decade-long discrimination against the Orientals by the Labor Party. Then came the pact with Egypt, and I hoped that this would usher in peace with the other Arab states. Living with Arabs comes naturally to me. I never considered them my enemies. The reason my Oriental friends voted for Begin was that they thought of him as the strong man. As for me, I was disgusted with the fight against the Arabs, but I voted Likud because I thought of it as the party of the Sephardim. But I liked and understood the Arabs. They are not strangers. I felt closer to them than to many an immigrant from Poland or Russia.

The illusion of many of the people here that all Jews are one, regardless of where they're from, is one of the most ridiculous misconceptions. Why should a Jew from the Caucasus be closer to me than an Arab from North Africa?

If the majority here ever turns this into a religious state I'll be among the first to leave. First Israeli, then Jew, not the other way round. I get along very well with nonreligious Arabs. They think the way I do and our cultural backgrounds are also similar. An Orthodox Jew is as alien to me as a devout Italian Catholic.

The State of Israel is more important to me than a country of the Jews. This country should be open to all, a democratic country in the Near East. That's what I believe in. Israel may be the only democratic country in the Near East, but it does not grant all its inhabitants full citizenship rights. It is a mixed society, and that's something that can't be changed anymore. But on the other hand, the Oriental and Arab segments are as important an element of the state—or perhaps an even more important one—as the religious Jewish sector, and that opens the door to an opportunity for change.

And then there's the political exploitation of the Holocaust. Jews are permitted to do whatever they want because they're the living victims. You would think that the Holocaust might serve as a reminder that here we have the opportunity to live in harmony with others. On the contrary: the Holocaust is cited as proof that we Jews are different from anyone else. The uniqueness of the extermination of the Jews also makes them into unique beings. Let us stop likening every injustice, every mass murder, to the Holocaust. A people that is afraid of being deprived of the uniqueness of its own extermination may have the right to consider itself chosen, but only for extermination.

I know, I have no right to talk. I didn't lose anybody in the Holocaust. My parents are not certified survivors. But sometimes I feel like the son of an Arab or a German who is constantly being reminded of the Holocaust. It is the threat which everyone feels entitled to use. Whoever criticizes Israel is immediately called a Nazi. Arafat is of course compared to Hitler; the intifada was organized by the Nazis; and the policies of the Arab countries are just like the Nazis'. How can we expect to enter into a new era, a new political direction and development, if we constantly compare everything to a terrible event of the past?

It's insane to look at every opponent, including every political opponent, as someone who wants to destroy the

Jews. How can we ever create a tolerant society? How can you expect to respect and esteem someone even though he doesn't agree with you if you compare him to a mass murderer, or to somebody who condones mass murder?

Every dignitary who comes to Tel Aviv is immediately taken to Yad Vashem, to the Holocaust Museum. Is that what we're proud of? After forty years of Israel we take them to see the nearly successful extermination of our people! I can't stand this lachrymose self-indulgence. Mine was a proud family in Morocco. I would also like to feel pride here, in my new home.

ALON

We're a big family—my father's brothers and sisters as well as my mother's, and lots of cousins and their uncles, aunts, children, and grandchildren. All in all, we're quite a clan. But none of us elected being related to one another. We were all born into it, and we all know everybody's business, what they do, and especially what they have. And relations between those who have more and those who have less are liable to get a little touchy. The most respected family members are the haves who give to the have-nots. We have plenty of takers but not so many givers, even if the ratio of haves to have-nots is about even.

Guilt feelings are the bread and butter of our family. There's always somebody in this vast circle who feels insulted. I was exposed to this for years at home and I still have the scars to show for it. My father lived in constant fear that he might unwittingly have insulted some aunt or uncle. In the long run this sort of fear can kill you. The richer the aunt or uncle in question, the greater the guilt feelings. Poverty wasn't what made us edgy, and it also wasn't worry over whether those who hadn't made it were getting the help they needed. No, that wasn't it. Pleasing the rich relatives, that's what mattered. Money was the most important thing, and it was on everyone's mind. Who had what, who had more, who had less. The millionaires were the somebodies, and those who weren't had a hard time being somebodies.

My parents also dreamed of becoming rich, but everything they undertook went wrong. In our house the Jewish dream of successful deal-making was fated to remain just that, a chapter in our collection of Jewish fairy tales. We didn't make any deals, or if so, only bad ones. My parents weren't the only failures in this family of successes. There were two groups, the ones who'd made it and the ones who hadn't. And those who'd made it despised one another. When the family got together on special occasions like weddings, the main topic was the business failures. As for me, I preferred the poor relatives, the failures; they were nicer.

I grew up and went to school in Jerusalem. My father first worked in a filling station, later he leased it, then he went bankrupt, after which he went to work in another filling station, and eventually he leased that one. He always wanted to be his own boss, but he turned out to be his own worst boss. Mother looked after the house. Her maternal feelings were a saving grace, although they often were too much of a good thing. She is a tall, strong woman, with shapely arms that nobody ever got to see because she kept them covered. All that mattered to her was that we children should eat well, not catch cold, and find a good Jewish husband or wife. I never worried about my weight, whether I was skinny or fat, but my sister was very upset about having food pushed at her. She was beautiful, and everybody was sure that she'd marry well. But she kept putting on weight, and so it wasn't easy for her to find the nice rich Jewish man my parents dreamed about.

Our family is quite religious. All laws are rigidly observed—kosher food, keeping the Sabbath. The reason for all this strict observance is a combination of bad conscience and fear. My parents are more afraid that a relative might see them drive a car on the Sabbath than of the transgression itself. Their religion was always more in the nature of a commitment entered into because of neighbors and relatives.

Father of course went to synagogue on Friday night, whether he wanted to or not, and naturally we all gathered around the table for the kiddush even if we were sick of the whole damn family. And Mother, she spent all Friday cooking even though she might have preferred reading a book. But they went on with their professions of piety. Father said kiddush, we children forced ourselves to eat more than we wanted just to get it over with and put an end to this embarrassing meal.

Saturdays were a nightmare. Things improved when we finally got a remote control, so we could at least turn the TV on. And we spent this sacred day, which the family is supposed to celebrate together, in front of that box without setting foot outdoors.

When the Sabbath finally ended I was able to relax. Those few short hours between nightfall and bedtime were my entire weekend. Sunday it was back to school. When the other children told of all the exciting things they'd done on Saturday, our one free day, all I could think of was having sat in front of the TV instead of playing with the other kids outside. What a life!

Worse still were the High Holy Days, when our observances seemed endless. It was like being locked up for a week, like being taken away from the world and incarcerated.

In thinking back on my childhood I remember our religious observances as torment, and everything having to do with religion as a horror. I had an almost manic desire to get away from home as soon as I was finished with school. Now, many years later, I often regret that I didn't have a less tortured relationship to religion.

The day after I graduated from high school I left home. I didn't care how I would manage. All I wanted was to get out of that prison. I moved to Tel Aviv to look for a job, but my freedom was short-lived. The army soon came after me. I was still in the military when the family began to worry about finding the right girl for me. Those dear relatives, they all worried about me. Every time I came home on leave I'd find some shy girl sitting there, not knowing what to do with herself. Of course it was all completely accidental. The girl just happened to be the daughter of rich Mr. So-and-So, and of course, she was beautiful and talented. Actually, they were all quite nice, but oh so boring, sitting there silently and smiling. They'd probably been told to smile and not talk.

I got out of the army, still single. I didn't want to go to college. All I wanted was finally to make some money and enjoy life in Tel Aviv.

I got a job in a restaurant, not exactly fun, but it was a beginning, and I was able to support myself and live by myself. The first few weeks in Tel Aviv were like one big adventure. I had moved away from all that suffocating religiosity, away from boring Jerusalem and the army, to a metropolis. Friday nights here were the polar opposite of Fridays at home. The city exploded. The streets and cafés were jammed, people were dancing in the streets, disco music was everywhere. Thousands of young people strolled along the beach promenade. Could this still be

Israel, I asked myself, the Holy Land of the Jews? I was ecstatic, drunk with youth and excitement, trying to make up for everything I had missed.

More and more I got away from religion. I lost the last shred of respect for the pious when my girlfriend, a licensed masseuse, told me about all those religious men who'd call up for an appointment, making sure that no one else was around. When they came they'd run through the waiting room and strip without first taking a shower. And as soon as she began to massage their soft, flabby bodies they started to make suggestive requests. After all, a woman in her profession would surely agree to anything. My girlfriend said she laughed out loud the first time that happened. There they lay, these pious believers with beards and sidelocks, dreaming of forbidden pleasures.

Ultimately I became fed up with my restaurant job and took one in a hospital kitchen. The work wasn't better, but at least the people I worked with were more interesting. And I also changed my opinion about religious people. There were young pious women working there who, because of their religion, were exempt from military service. You wouldn't believe how dedicated and industrious they were.

At the hospital I met a Jewish woman doctor from Vienna who'd come to Israel for postgraduate studies. She was different from the Israelis. There was something sensitive about her, not so loud and uncivil as the women here. Israeli women are a combination of mother and grandmother. They don't grow up unless their mothers order them to. They are probably the most beautiful fighters in the world. Where else can you find such beautiful women soldiers? But who would try to conquer such a beauty? And you certainly don't want to possess her.

Well, Ruth from Vienna was entirely different. She kept

on talking about her problem with Judaism, with the Holocaust, with the neo-Nazis, subjects which I knew about only from the papers. The Holocaust was never a big issue in our family. We hadn't lost anybody in the camps. All our family had settled here earlier. Actually, I found the preoccupation with the Holocaust rather unpleasant—those annual memorials, the school trips to Auschwitz where we stood around without wanting to understand it. And those constant admonitions to remember the victims. I felt closer to the victims of the Lebanon war than to the victims of the Holocaust.

But Ruth talked like a philosopher. How she could talk! Not like any Israeli I knew. For the first time I got an inkling of that fascinating combination of German background and Judaism. The German immigrants we used to call Yekkes were dying out. By the time I came to the hospital there was only one German professor still there. He spoke with a German accent even though he'd been here for decades.

After a year in the hospital Ruth persuaded me to come to Vienna with her. Ours was a strange relationship. She was older than I, more mature, and most certainly more intelligent. I often wondered what she saw in me. We talked English with each other. I think what she liked about me was my sense of humor. When she was with me she laughed a lot. I wasn't quite sure why I felt attracted to her, but the idea of going to Vienna certainly appealed to me. Her parents glowed when they met me. Later I found out why. Because there weren't all that many Jewish men in Vienna, Ruth was always running around with goyim, and her parents didn't like that. Her father had arranged for her to go to Tel Aviv in the hope that his little daughter would come back with an acceptable husband. I was it, and if I wasn't exactly the ideal man, at least I was Jewish.

At first I wasn't bothered by any of this. We lived in her parents' house in the attic in a room with bath. The house had a solarium, a sauna, and a pool. Paradise. I'd sleep till noon, then spend an hour in the pool, and after that watch TV until Ruth came home from the hospital. I studied the language, and after only a few weeks became fluent in German. My Yiddish helped a lot.

By and by I began to get bored. I tried to make friends, but my ventures into the outside world were disastrous. I found myself in a strange setting, away from the snug house, among frustrated, aggressive people. My idea was just to be of help, do the shopping, but I caused nothing but trouble. If I touched an apple or put back a rotten tomato, the shopkeepers would get furious, and when they saw they were dealing with a foreigner things got even worse.

The next few months were nightmarish. I became paranoid; I felt I was surrounded by Jew-hating, drunken Nazis who were out to kill me. When I took a taxi I waited for what was sure to come—the driver's rantings about foreigners, gays, or Jews.

And there was the almost pathological antireligious attitude of Ruth's parents. I was of course glad that I no longer had to observe all the laws, but at Ruth's house they had a Christmas tree, sang "Silent Night," exchanged presents, and on Christmas Eve we all went to Saint Stephen's Square to listen to the bells.

Were these people still Jews? I asked myself. What defines their Judaism? Is it their fight against the primitive goyim? Are they Jews only because they are persecuted, and what will be left of their Judaism if one day they stop feeling like victims? I asked Ruth's father, who was in the jewelry business, whether he was going to close his shop on Yom Kippur. He couldn't understand why I would even ask such a question, nor why I fasted.

I knew things couldn't go on this way. I tried to persuade Ruth to move out, to get our own apartment and live our own lives. I wanted to get a job and maybe go to college. I was tired of life as a male housekeeper. She agreed, and we moved out. A couple of weeks later I happened to find out that the building in which we got the apartment belonged to Ruth's father.

In the next few weeks I tried to make contact with various Jewish institutions in Vienna. I went to discussions about Israel and Jewish life. Another disappointment. These talks about Israel were like debates among prophets. Everyone knew exactly who'd done the right thing and who hadn't. Everyone had an opinion, and they couldn't understand why the Israelis couldn't agree among themselves. The longer I was in Vienna the sillier all that fine talk I had admired Ruth for in Israel seemed to me. There's nobody who can say nothing as beautifully as Viennese Jews.

I couldn't stomach life in Vienna, and after almost a year I returned to Israel. The Jews of Vienna make believe they live in an atmosphere of persecution. They try to make life interesting for themselves by pretending that they're surrounded by enemies, like playing hide-and-seek with old and new Nazis. And when they actually come across one they carry on. I too became infected by this hysteria.

What problems do they actually have? It's ridiculous. Their life there is unpalatable, not dangerous. The Viennese are coarse, stupid, and insensitive, but to try to make that into a potential pogrom is perverse.

My thoughts kept going back to Israel, to the wounded soldiers in the hospital, to the families that had lost only

sons, to the children who had lost fathers, to the young
men in wheelchairs. And here they sit in Vienna, those
poor Jews, and complain, and don't know what to do with
all their money. And when they get really bored they discuss
Israel and dish out no end of good advice and prophecies.
I wish them a real face-to-face encounter with some bel-
ligerent anti-Semites so they won't forget completely that
they're Jews.

Now I'm back in Israel. Nothing has changed, and that's
nice. I can live in my country full of crazy Jews the way I
choose, strictly Orthodox in a religious quarter or so assimilated that I can go dancing on the Sabbath and eat
sweet-and-sour pork in a Chinese restaurant, or, like some
of my friends, have a dinner party on Yom Kippur. Everything can be done. But at least I'm living in the present.
The threat posed by the Arabs is real and concrete. I might
be killed by a bomb in a bus, or one of my brothers in the
army might be killed by a bullet. That's the reality we live
with here. Nowhere else are world events such a tangible
presence as here.

The Jews of Vienna undoubtedly are wonderful people
—educated, well-read, witty, intelligent. But their psyche
is sick. They no longer have any enemies, so they go looking
for them. And if they don't find them they sit around and
cry over the past.

RIFKA

I have seven brothers and one sister, and I grew up in a hothouse atmosphere—spoiled and the center of attention. It was wonderful. My family is very traditional. My brothers went either to Torah schools or religious boarding schools. In the end all of them turned their back on religion. I was the only one who didn't attend a religious school. Why, I don't know. A miracle, perhaps? Suppose I'd gone to a religious school, would I now be very Orthodox or the opposite, like my brothers? I was spared all of this. When I left home I also left all tradition behind.

My mother, who worked as a cook in a restaurant in Safed, had bragged to her boss about me, about what a good student I was, whereupon the woman asked me to help her seven-year-old daughter with her schoolwork. I was twelve at the time. I went there every day, and six months later I was also looking after her eight-month-old son, and not long after that I began to sleep over at their house. It was a rich family, and now I always had enough money of my own and didn't have to ask my parents for anything. My sister was very sheltered. She didn't have nearly as much freedom as I.

My parents' life centered on their children. All of us at home had to pitch in. The boys were responsible for keeping the house clean, and when Mother was working Father did the cooking. And all of them spoiled me. My brothers brought me presents and took me along to the movies. They paid more attention to me than my parents. Even now some of them, particularly the ones who live in the United States, still send me gifts. For the holidays the entire family assembles here, however far away they may be. Everybody comes.

My parents are from Morocco. Father was twenty when he married Mother. She was thirteen. It was an arranged marriage. My mother, the daughter of a rabbi, had no say. Both my parents' families were well-to-do. My paternal grandfather was a doctor, a kind of miracle healer. He practiced herbal medicine and was said to be able to straighten out bent limbs and perform other such miraculous feats.

When my parents came to Israel in 1956 they went to live in Jerusalem. From there they went to a moshav, and finally they came to Safed. Safed is quite a religious community. On the Sabbath everything comes to a stop; there are no cars on the street and no open shops. The religious leaders succeeded in getting all stores to close up on the Sabbath, even those of nonobservant owners. And on weekdays the religious population is swelled by people coming to visit the graves of wonder rabbis buried there. As is bound to happen in this sort of imposed religiosity, we all tried to break away. My sister, who is still at home, has a hard time.

When I came of draft age I wanted to go to the Nahal. My parents were against any military service for me. A pious girl isn't supposed to become a soldier. But all my brothers were in elite units, and so I didn't want to ask for an exemption. One of my brothers, a paratrooper, ran into some bad luck. They ordered him to get a haircut, but he must have gotten lost on the way. They caught up with him, and he spent four weeks in jail.

I came to the air force, not the Nahal. I was thrilled. Wild and undisciplined as I was, I'd hoped to be in a combat outfit. Having spent all my life in the company of boys, I was not all that enthusiastic about being in a girls' outfit. But what kind of jobs do you think they give to women in the air force? Secretaries to officers. I told them that's the last thing I had in mind, and so they offered me a different job, as a salesclerk in the commissary. I made the best of a bad bargain. When word got around that that's where I'd be working, the soldiers lined up to have me wait on them. I was an attraction, but after a month this too became boring. Once again I tried to get to a combat outfit, but it didn't work. They sent me to a computer course, and after that I of course became a secretary. However, it was an interesting job having to do with aircraft production and technical matters.

It wasn't a bad life at all. Weekends we flew to Elath and at night we went out in Tel Aviv. I also took a course in sports training, but I didn't get out of my unit, for purely military reasons, naturally. One of the officers had fallen in love with me and refused to approve my transfer to another unit.

When my tour of duty was over they wanted me to stay, but I didn't feel like it. I didn't like the conformity. And always wearing the same thing. After all, I'm an individual, so why can't I wear something individual? I was repeatedly called down for not wearing the uniform as prescribed. I like a more personal touch, even when in uniform.

After leaving the army I tried my hand at various other jobs. I worked in a boutique, then as a waitress, and also tended bar. I made lots of money in tips. That's what I'm best at, getting money out of people. After that I became a travel guide, taking tourists across the Jordan in rubber boats. That was exciting and wild, paddling across white water and waterfalls. Later we also tried crossing in canoes. It took five hours to go from Jordan to the Sea of Nazareth.

Now I'm back in Tel Aviv working as a nursemaid. It's hard work, from seven in the morning to six at night. I make a lot of money because rent and food are free. But God knows how long I'll be able to stand it. I'd like to save some money and visit New York. Three of my brothers are in America and they keep on writing me how exciting life there is. They don't plan to stay there; making some money and then coming back here wouldn't be such a bad idea. The face cream that costs me about fifty dollars here costs two dollars over there. I also wouldn't mind going to France and Germany, at least long enough to learn the language.

My parents keep harping on marriage, but I'm not yet ready to settle down and have a family. It doesn't matter what the topic of conversation is, it always boils down to this: If only you'd finally get yourself a husband. I'm sure I'd get lots of presents if I were to marry, but I'm not going to do it just for the gifts.

I'm not a typical Israeli. I look a little different, I dress a little different, and I am a little different. Maybe I'm a little crazy. But one day I'm sure to meet a man I like and have lots of children. Then I'll dress like all the other women here, light candles Friday night, and keep a neat house. I'll go shopping, gossip with the neighbors, wait for the children to come home from school, and take good care of my husband and keep him happy so that he'll like staying home with the family. I'll become an ordinary Israeli woman, and I look forward to it.

RAN

I was born in 1950 in Brashov, Rumania. My father called himself Visendan. Having been born in Visen, he took Visendan as his cover name in the Communist anti-Nazi Underground. His family name was Friedman, and our name now, Fry, is a shortened form of that original name. By dropping his Underground name when we came here in 1970, my father was manifesting his desire to return to his roots, but not completely, only halfway. He now thinks of himself as an Israeli, not necessarily as a Jew, and so he changed Friedman to Fry.

Our life in Rumania in the postwar years was very good. After all, Father had helped defeat the Nazis, and the regime then in power embodied his political ideals. He became party secretary, and later was appointed to a high position in Bucharest. We were well off, with a private chauffeur and a nice apartment. As part of the upper crust we lacked for nothing, and Father thought that was only as it should be. After all, hadn't he risked his life during the war?

But then, in 1958, everything came crashing down. Within weeks all Jewish activists were expelled from the party. The Jewish doctors' trials were getting under way in the Soviet Union, and the Party purge of foreign elements and Jews was spreading to the Eastern Bloc countries. Father was in shock. He, the decorated Communist resistance fighter who never thought of himself as a Jew, was now out because he was a Jew. We hadn't lived like Jews. We were Communists, and a Communist is neither a Rumanian nor a Jew, but a member of the world proletariat. We were still so naive and deluded that we didn't realize that what was happening was a campaign aimed specifically against Jews, not as alleged a drive to root out harmful elements. And if Jewish party members were caught up in this hunt for those who had erred, it was only as part of an evidence-gathering process. This campaign didn't raise our Jewish consciousness one iota. Nonetheless, Father lost his job. They bugged our phone and put us under secret police surveillance.

I was then eight years old. My parents sent me away to an aunt in a town near the Hungarian border. They told me that because Father was out of a job they now had no money and had become pariahs, and therefore I'd be better off with my aunt. I stayed there for a year. My sisters remained at home. My aunt was also a Communist. Her husband had been a partisan and had fought with the Russians. They refused to admit that our misfortune had anything to do with being Jewish.

Slowly things began to return to normal. Father was allowed to work and we had enough to get by. In 1969 we began to toy with the idea of emigrating to Israel. It's not that we were excluded from society. At high school and later at the university I met other Jewish students, the children of Communists who had been reinstated to positions in the party hierarchy. We stuck together not because we were Jews but because we were a little different. That was the basis of our closeness. I can't remember a Jewish community in our milieu, other than the students who just felt drawn to each other. And not all in our group were necessarily Jews. Rather, what we had in common was our social class. People who'd lost their posts were culturally isolated from other groups of the society.

When Ceausescu came to power, in 1961, he tried to woo all sectors and offered to rehabilitate Father. But he'd had enough. He preferred his job at the factory, and he stayed there until we left. When he turned down the government's offer they gave him a pension, 50 percent more than he was making as an engineer, and so at least we were in good shape financially.

Actually Father was the one who was eager to leave. When he was young he had risked everything for this new state, and now, after what they had done to him, he saw no reason for staying. He must have felt that this part of his life was over and that he wanted to make a fresh start. His children were on the threshold of their careers and their prospects were bleak. Young people in Rumania had no future. Jews had a choice; they could leave. We no longer felt we belonged, and so we chose to go to Israel.

My father had family there, brothers and sisters, which made Israel the obvious choice. We experienced culture shock when we suddenly found ourselves amidst nothing but Jews. It takes time getting used to. And the political openness was a still greater shock. When I heard people tell jokes about Golda Meir in public places my impulse was to hide so as not to have to witness this sort of political insult. It takes a while to get rid of these fears. Maybe one never does. Respect for authority is so deeply ingrained that it becomes part of one's personality. That's how we were brought up. It's impossible to adjust completely to this casual attitude toward authority. Perhaps my children will one day.

When I arrived in Israel I let my hair grow. I couldn't have done it in Rumania. There the police dragged you to the barber. I went to Elath to become part of the hippie culture, to smoke pot. It took me about three months to learn enough Hebrew to get by. Lots of people here also speak English and French. My first foreign language is French, then English, and then Hebrew.

Coming here was the realization of my dream of freedom. I felt at home right away. With one stroke I put Rumania out of my mind completely. I wrote to nobody. I wanted to erase this part of my past, not so much because I was angry over the way they'd treated Father, but rather to help me come to terms with my new situation. Israel meant freedom, Elath meant freedom, Rumania was the other world, the gray prison from which I'd finally been released.

I stayed in Elath for a couple of months, long enough to get my bearings. In Rumania I had been studying civil engineering, the only field in which Jews had a chance. I had ruled out philosophy because it would have meant Marxist philosophy, and I couldn't have made a living in politics, so civil engineering was the answer. When I got here I thought I'd continue in that field, but after only a semester I realized that that's not what I wanted, and so I switched to psychology and art history. Then came the army, and after I got out it was back to art. I became a teacher. When I turned thirty—I was by then the father of a son—I thought that I'd better do something about making a living. I studied computer science, and that's how I earn my living now.

I had no difficulty adjusting to Israeli society, though it

was a gradual process. At Elath I'd made friends with both foreign and local hippies. At the university my friends were largely immigrants. Nobody automatically becomes part of Israeli society. Israelis are not a homogeneous group; they come from all parts of the globe. I always felt that whatever it is that makes an Israeli, I can live with it. I had no problems. The idiosyncrasies such as their directness, offhandedness, rudeness, don't bother me. On the contrary, when I go abroad I miss that directness, and I know others who feel the same. That directness breaks down all barriers. And there isn't that constant fear as in Rumania. My childhood was made up of rules. Here anything goes.

The first time I was called up for three months army training was while in college. That was difficult. At the end of those three months I went back to school to complete my studies. After graduating, I did my full army service, which turned out not to be all that difficult. Israeli society allows you to move step by step. If you want to move gradually, to sort of grow into things, you can do it. The thought of leaving here never even crosses my mind. I've become a part of this country even though I know that materially I could do better somewhere else, for example, in the United States.

Religion didn't exist for me in Rumania. It just wasn't part of our lives. The family was our religion. But when I got to Israel I began to get interested in religion, mostly in meditation. At first, I grew enthusiastic about all types of mysticism, particularly Hinduism. Of course, that didn't exactly bring me closer to Judaism, but still it meant a kind of religious upheaval for me. After all the vaunted objectivity of Rumanian communism, I was an easy mark for mysticism and religion.

The fact that my father didn't try to stop me came as a

surprise. He was and remains a confirmed atheist, while I consider myself a believer. Perhaps I am my father's offering to God, the prayer he himself cannot bring himself to recite. This has become my self-assigned task.

Nobody came to me and tried to convert me. I wouldn't have responded. I'd had my fill of indoctrination back in Rumania. I know people here have reservations about Hinduism and meditation, but I was old enough to make up my own mind. I was twenty-one when I came here. Also, I wasn't your typical Jewish youngster, the product of a Jewish home. I was a Jew by birth but not by education. I hadn't been raised with a Jewish consciousness. I had no Jewish guilt, no parents to punish by turning my back on religious observance. There can be no doubt about my being an Israeli, but I still don't feel Jewish. There's a difference between being a Jew and being an Israeli, just as being French and being Catholic are not synonymous.

Some people say that the Jewish religion is the glue that holds the country together. I disagree. I think it is the Jewish tradition. Jewish life does not necessarily mean a religious life. There is a difference between Judaism and religious Judaism. Being an Israeli means being a citizen of this country. Nobody here is an outsider. Everywhere else Jews are outsiders, but not here. Feeling secure is a basic human need. Here I, a Hindu who was born a Jew and had to flee from a communist country where he was persecuted as a Jew, feel secure.

Many people who came here from Poland go back for a visit now that things have changed there. I have no desire to visit Rumania. That chapter of my life is closed. I don't have roots there. If my children one day should want to visit Rumania I wouldn't stop them.

I know I shouldn't be so laid-back about the future of my children. The conflict with the Palestinians, the danger of war with our Arab neighbors, is all too real, and not everything here is wonderful. Still, there's no other place in which I'd rather raise my children. I see no alternative. When I speak of security I don't mean an easy life or material wealth. Rather, I mean not feeling like a stranger, like a curiosity, to be able to take being secure for granted. And that's what I gained when I decided to stay here. Perhaps we all have territorial instincts, like animals that mark off their domain. Here I feel that I am in mine. It is my country. That is how I feel.

ABOUT THE AUTHOR

Peter Sichrovsky was born in Vienna to Jewish parents. A chemist and physicist before he embarked on a successful writing career, he is the author of a book about drugs which became a bestseller in Austria and Germany. Two of his other books, *Strangers in Their Own Land* (1986) and *Born Guilty* (1988) have been published in the United States. A dramatization of *Born Guilty* was produced at the Arena Stage in Washington, D.C., in 1991. He is now the Southeast Asia correspondent of the *Süddeutsche Zeitung*, stationed in New Delhi.